What's Wrong

What's Wrong

A Survey of American Satisfaction and Complaint

Everett Carll Ladd and
Karlyn H. Bowman

The AEI Press

Publisher for the American Enterprise Institute
Washington, D.C.

The Roper Center for Public Opinion Research

University of Connecticut
Storrs, Connecticut

1998

This volume is a joint research project and publication of the American Enterprise Institute for Public Policy Research, Washington, D.C., and the Roper Center for Public Opinion Research, University of Connecticut, Storrs, Connecticut.

Available in the United States from the AEI Press, c/o Publisher Resources Inc., 1224 Heil Quaker Blvd., P.O. Box 7001, La Vergne, TN 37086-7001. To order, call toll free 1-800-269-6267. Distributed outside the United States by arrangement with Eurospan, 3 Henrietta Street, London WC2E 8LU England.

Library of Congress Cataloging-in-Publication Data

Ladd, Everett Carll.
What's wrong : a survey of American satisfaction and complaint / Everett Carll Ladd and Karlyn H. Bowman.
p. cm.
Includes bibliographical references.
ISBN 0-8447-3955-3 (paper : alk. paper)
1. United States—Social conditions—1980- 2. United States—Economic conditions—1981- 3. United States—Politics and government—1993- 4. Public opinion polls—United States.
I. Bowman, Karlyn H. II. Title.
HN59.2.L33 1998
306'.0973—DC21

98-4046
CIP

1 2 3 4 5 6 7 8 9 10

THE AEI PRESS
Publisher for the American Enterprise Institute
1150 Seventeenth Street, N.W.
Washington, D.C. 20036

Printed in the United States of America

Contents

Acknowledgments vii

1 Introduction 1

2 The Status of American Democracy 5

3 Sense of Self, Sense of Nation 23

4 Opportunity 51

5 Politics and Government 73

6 Confidence in Institutions 115

7 A Summing Up 148

Appendix: A Note on the Tables 151

About the Authors 153

Acknowledgments

Melissa Knauer single-handedly undertook the herculean task of compiling the data in the tables and checking their accuracy. This involved lengthy searches of on-line data archives such as the one Everett Ladd heads at the Roper Center at the University of Connecticut, but it also required checking original survey releases for backup data. She has worked tirelessly on this project for many months, always with extraordinary attention to detail and with good humor.

In addition, we are very grateful for the help of individuals at some of the major survey organizations. Maura A. Strausberg, the head librarian at Gallup, knows the Gallup collection inside and out. Over and over again, she took time from her work to help us with this project. Erin Fowler at Roper Starch Worldwide searched the organization's database to help us fill in points. Dana Blanton at the Opinion Dynamics/Fox News poll updated several questions for us. Susan Lilley at Cambridge Reports/Research International also helped provide data for a few key tables. We hope they benefit from this as much as we have benefited from their help.

Major survey organizations such as Gallup, Harris, CBS News/*New York Times,* ABC News/*Washington Post,* NBC News/*Wall Street Journal,* Yankelovich Partners, the *Los Angeles Times,* the Pew Research Center (formerly the Times Mirror Center), Roper Starch Worldwide, Cambridge Reports/Research International, and Wirthlin Worldwide have supplied their data to us on a regular basis. Bringing together the work they have done is small payment for the data they have provided us over the years.

What's Wrong

CHAPTER 1
Introduction

In 1979, after reviewing a large collection of public opinion polls that documented a broad decline in confidence in key institutions and leaders, one of the authors of this volume wrote that Americans "are just about as dissatisfied as they should be . . . Americans know they occupy a very fortunate society. . . . They like their society and its institutions. They want to preserve them. But they don't think recent performance has been up to snuff."[1] Everett Ladd's assessment was not the first poll-based appraisal of its kind. In a review of public opinion data in 1971, Albert Cantril and Charles Roll wrote that Americans were clearly troubled about the state of their country. The authors described a "pervasive mood of disquiet" and argued that "traditional optimism about the nation's steady progress has faltered."[2]

Cantril and Roll's downbeat assessment of the national mood was tempered by what they described as people's "sense of accomplishment in terms of their personal aspirations" as well as optimism about their personal futures. Ladd also reflected on the dissonance in the data between people's optimism about their personal lives and their pessimism about the country.

Ladd argued that we should stop worrying about how confident people are, in part because they were not saying anything very alarming. The public critique of national performance was not likely to shatter the system; it was simply one of "spotty performance by leaders and institutions."

---

1. Everett C. Ladd, *Public Opinion*, October/November 1979, p. 27.
2. Albert H. Cantril and Charles W. Roll, *Hopes and Fears of the American People* (New York: Universe Books, 1971).

Serious consequences *would* follow if the public were deeply dissatisfied. It is hard to sustain central institutions and transmit ideals to future generations if citizens lack faith in those institutions or ideals. With much of the world embracing ideas the United States has long proclaimed and admiring the recent performance of the U.S. economy, it would be tragic indeed if we were losing faith in the system. But that is not the case.

Our argument in this volume is certainly not that things are A-OK. There is much that is wrong. But we believe the evidence is not as broadly negative as is often suggested. Furthermore, we would like to offer a good word for dissatisfaction. To some extent, people are always dissatisfied. This condition should not necessarily alarm us; dissatisfaction can be an engine for change.

We think of this book as a layman's guide to the mood of America. Our aim here is to present a fuller picture of arenas of satisfaction and dissatisfaction in America than has been offered before. We begin this examination in chapter 2 by looking at how people assess the idea of America. The foundations of our system appear solid. In chapter 3, we listen to how people say they are doing, and then we compare that perception with how people think the nation is faring. The bullishness about personal life is impressive. The mixed assessment of national life in the polls seems to be on target.

Much has been written about opportunity in America, and in chapter 4, we look at the robustness of this core idea. Do people still believe that opportunity is present for themselves, their children, or their countrymen? Related to the notion of opportunity are our views about the American Dream. Data on the status of the promise to which the "dream" refers extend back barely more than a decade, and the picture they provide is more than a little muddled. Drawing sweeping conclusions from the few questions about the demise of a sense of high promise is premature and unwarranted.

Chapter 5 puts Americans' views about politics and government under the microscope. The data show that a healthy skepticism toward politics and politicians has existed at least as far back as surveys have attempted to tap it. That does not mean it is healthy today, of course. The public's evaluation of current government performance is largely negative; we are far from satisfied with the way many—but not all—our central institutions are performing (chapter 6). A separate note on the tables located in the appendix to the book explains how we treated other data.

Polls

Before we begin this data review, a word about the polls. We live in a poll-infused culture. For the most part, that is good, for polls can tell us a great deal about the society. Viewed over the past sixty years, our numbers narrative is rich and compelling. The polls, though, can have biases of their own, and not just those stemming from the familiar sources of error in surveys. The following examples illustrate. In 1945, when there were only a few pollsters in the field, the word *lie* was used for the first time in a survey question. Perhaps surprisingly, from the early 1970s through Nixon's resignation in 1974, the word was used only a handful of times in surveys. During the Iran-contra investigation in 1986 and 1987, when far more pollsters were practicing the craft, *lie* was used in survey questions eighty-eight times. The pejorative *politics as usual* was used three times in the 1940s, but not again until the 1970s; it was used many times in 1997 to describe campaign fundraising practices of both parties. We can find no references before 1988 to a politician's *hiding something*. Today, that question is asked routinely about politicians in the limelight.[3]

Most politics watchers would probably agree that politics is cleaner than it was a decade or two ago and that the propensity to lie has not changed much over time. Yet the impression conveyed by the polls is much more negative than what we would have come up with years ago when there were fewer polls and less a media-driven imperative to take a poll on every political pecadillo.

Much has been written about the negativity bias in the media, the tendency to cover stories that show how we as a society are falling short. Our purpose here is not to review the evidence on this point, but we believe that the pollsters, and particularly the pollsters associated with major media outlets, may be contributing to a distorted picture of the society. One of the tables in this volume shows that Americans have been asked more than a hundred times since 1958 how much of the time they trust the government in Washington to do what is right. Since 1974, majorities or pluralities have consistently said they trust the government only some or none of the time (table 5–20). It is important to know how

3. This effort to look at key words is imperfect at best. We searched the Roper Center's poll archive for these words. Although it is the most comprehensive historical database available, it does not include all the survey questions ever asked.

much people trust the government, of course, and we have no quarrel with asking this question regularly and reporting the results. But what if equal media attention had been given to people's responses to this statement, Whatever its faults, the United States still has the best system of government in the world—where large majorities have given the positive response? This question has been asked three times in the past seven years; the trust question has been asked forty-nine times in the past seven years.

In late May 1997, President Clinton participated in the fiftieth anniversary celebration of the Marshall Plan. Over the years, pollsters have asked many questions about attitudes toward Europe and the NATO alliance. Yet, during this consequential anniversary week, we found only one national survey that explored public attitudes toward the NATO alliance. The same week, a number of national pollsters posed questions about Paula Jones, Kelly Flinn, and Frank Gifford. The emphasis on the salacious makes us worry that the polls are adding to an overly negative picture of a society where there are clearly problems but just as clearly profound and deep satisfactions. This volume is a reminder that both perspectives abound.

CHAPTER 2

The Status of American Democracy

The data in this section demonstrate that the American ideology is fundamentally strong. There is scant evidence that people are ready to give up on the country's founding hopes or ideals or that we think them less practical than in the past. We begin by looking at some long trends on democratic fundamentals. Table 2–1 shows that in 1974, 87 percent of those surveyed by Gallup said they had "quite a lot" or "some" confidence in the future of the United States. When the question was last repeated in 1994, that number had edged downward, but an impressive 81 percent were still confident. Fewer than 20 percent in both years had very little or no confidence at all in the future of the United States.

In October 1973, Roper Starch Worldwide began asking people whether they were optimistic, pessimistic, or uncertain about the country's future (table 2–2). In 1973, 39 percent said they were generally optimistic; in 1994, when Roper Starch Worldwide last posed the question, 44 percent gave that response. The number who were generally pessimistic moved from 12 to 21 percent in the twenty-one-year time frame. Also shown in this table are questions from other survey organizations that ask more directly about optimism or pessimism about the future of the country. The responses are overwhelmingly positive.

A series of questions posed by Roper Starch Worldwide and Gallup for more than two decades shows no fundamental loss of confidence in the underpinnings of our democracy. People have almost always been more optimistic than pessimistic about the soundness of our economic system over the long run and about the way our leaders are chosen. In the one area that shows some change (views about our system of government and how well it works), the pessimistic contingent has grown from 15 to 34 percent over the twenty-three-year period (table 2–3). Tables 2–4 and 2–5 provide additional data on public perceptions of the durability and promise of the American system.

Table 2–6 reminds us that the can-do spirit, so much remarked on by historians and others, is still strong. In a 1997 Pew Research Center study, 71 percent of those surveyed completely or mostly agreed that "as Americans we can always find a way to solve our problems and get what we want." The urge to leave the country is almost nonexistent (table 2–7), and pride in the nation is strong (table 2–8). We rank the level of our personal freedom very high compared with the freedom people in other countries enjoy (table 2–9), and we think that "whatever its faults, the United States still has the best system of government in the world" (table 2–10). When asked about the country's greatness, we seem torn between "greatest" and "great" (table 2–11), and only a handful thinks other countries are better than our own. Responses to a question about the country's economic standing (also in this table) show that few people have written the country off.

The next three questions in this chapter do not deal with the fabric of our democracy but ask instead for responses about the current state of things. When we care deeply about something as we do about our democracy, we worry about it. These questions—and many others like them in the survey literature—underscore that point. They are also more likely than the other questions shown thus far to be influenced by current economic conditions, and the responses are more volatile. A question NBC News and the *Wall Street Journal* began asking in 1990 shows that majorities or near majorities since 1991 see America in a state of decline (table 2–12). A Gallup question with very uneven responses shows considerable dissatisfaction with the way democracy is working (table 2–13.) We are generally skeptical of questions that ask people to look into their crystal balls and predict the future, in part because the responses to those questions often turn out to be a proxy for our views of current conditions. Gallup's and Yankelovich's questions about the shape the country will be in in the year 2000 appear to reflect, for example, people's perceptions of the shape the country is in today. People were slightly more pessimistic in 1992 than they were when the question was asked again in May 1997 (table 2–14). Broader questions tend to show that majorities believe America's best days are ahead (table 2–15).

The final questions in this chapter tap a familiar feeling, the belief that things were better or that our circumstances were happier at some point in the past. Although we were not able to come up with matching questions, the ones that we have chosen show that the nostalgia impulse is strong and enduring (table 2–16). In 1939, for example, people told Gallup interviewers that Americans were happier and more content in the horse-and-buggy days. In 1994, those surveyed told Roper Starch Worldwide that the "good old days" were better than the present. In 1937, 50 percent worried that religion was losing influence. Sixty years later, in 1997, 60 percent also said it was losing its influence. A 1937 survey found 45 percent saying that sexual moral standards were worse than a generation ago (only 17 percent said they were better). Views about the deterioration of morality in our society are more emphatic in the late 1990s. In a Gallup question, 76 percent said that moral values were weaker than twenty-five years ago; only 7 percent said they were stronger. Americans are persistently anxious about the status of their institutions and ideals because they care deeply about them.

TABLE 2–1
CONFIDENCE IN THE FUTURE OF THE UNITED STATES, 1974–1994
(percent)

QUESTION: How much confidence do you have in the future of the United States—quite a lot, some, very little, or none at all?

	Quite a Lot	*Some*	*Very Little*	*None at All*
Apr. 1974	68	19	10	2
Aug. 1974	64	24	8	2
Aug. 1975	60	23	13	3
Mar. 1976	57	30	9	1
June 1986	76	19	4	1
May 1991	59	34	5	1
Aug. 1994	48	33	15	3

QUESTION: Would you tell me how much confidence you, yourself, have in the future of the United States—a great deal, quite a lot, some, or very little?

	Great Deal	*Quite a Lot*	*Some*	*Very Little*
June 1975[a]	49	26	16	7
Jan. 1977[a]	43	29	19	7
Apr. 1979[a, b]	45	27	17	8
Jan. 1987[b]	41	29	20	8
Mar. 1987	48	24	17	10
May 1988	47	30	14	6
Sept. 1988	45	28	17	8
Feb. 1991	48	27	17	7

a. Question prefaced with: "I am going to read you a list of institutions in American society . . . ."
b. One percent volunteered the response "none."
SOURCES: For first panel, surveys by the Gallup Organization (1974–1991) and Princeton Survey Research Associates for *Newsweek* (1994). For second panel, surveys by the Gallup Organization.

TABLE 2–2
OPTIMISM OR PESSIMISM ABOUT THE COUNTRY'S FUTURE, 1973–1996
(percent)

QUESTION: Now I'd like to ask how you feel about the future. Considering everything, would you say you feel generally optimistic about the future of our country or generally pessimistic or that you're uncertain about our country's future?

	Optimistic	*Pessimistic*	*Uncertain*
Oct. 1973	39	12	45
May 1974	41	15	41
Aug. 1974	41	13	42
Aug. 1975	43	15	40
May 1976	43	15	39
Feb. 1977	51	12	33
Aug. 1977	43	17	37
Feb. 1979	39	20	39
Aug. 1979	44	18	37
Feb. 1981	50	14	34
Feb. 1983	45	14	40
Sept. 1983	49	11	39
Feb. 1984	51	11	36
Feb. 1986	47	13	36
Oct. 1986	44	12	42
Feb. 1987	45	15	38
Feb. 1988	46	16	35
Feb. 1989	53	13	29
Feb. 1991	51	13	34
Feb. 1994	44	21	32

(Table continues)

TABLE 2–2 (continued)

QUESTION: Would you say that you are optimistic or pessimistic about the future of this country?
QUESTION: In general, are you optimistic or pessimistic about this country's future?
QUESTION: Are you optimistic about the future of America?
QUESTION: Please tell me whether you strongly agree, somewhat agree, somewhat disagree or strongly disagree with the following statement . . . I am optimistic about America's future.

	Poll	*Optimistic*	*Pessimistic*
Dec. 1983	ABC	73	21
Sept. 1988	NBC/*WSJ*	77	13
Jan. 1992	ORC/MPT	75	23
Aug. 1994	Luntz	64	32
May 1996	ABC	70	27
Nov. 1996	Luntz	67	28

QUESTION: What is your outlook for the United States during the next 20 years? Would you say it is very optimistic, optimistic, pessimistic, or very pessimistic?

	Very Optimistic	*Optimistic*	*Pessimistic*	*Very Pessimistic*
1978	8	55	23	6
1991	10	69	14	4

SOURCES: For first panel, surveys by Roper Starch Worldwide, latest that of February 1994. For second panel, surveys by ABC News, NBC News/*Wall Street Journal,* Opinion Research Corporation for Maryland Public Television, and Luntz Research Companies. For third panel, surveys by the Gallup Organization, latest that of May 1991.

TABLE 2–3: Optimism or Pessimism about Different Aspects of the Country's Future, 1974–1997 (percent)

Question: As I read a list of items, please say whether you feel generally optimistic about it as far as the future is concerned, generally pessimistic about it, or uncertain about it.

	Aug. 1974	*Aug. 1975*	*Feb. 1977*	*Aug. 1977*	*Feb. 1979*	*Feb. 1981*	*Feb. 1983*	*Oct. 1986*[a]	*Feb. 1988*	*Feb. 1991*	*Jan. 1992*[a]	*Jan. 1993*[a]	*Feb. 1994*	*Feb. 1995*	*Mar. 1996*	*Mar. 1997*
Soundness of our economic system over the long run																
Optimistic	43	45	46	40	38	47	46	—	42	44	—	—	43	35	47	43
Pessimistic	21	21	20	23	26	22	22	—	25	21	—	—	26	35	23	30
Uncertain	30	29	29	31	31	29	26	—	27	31	—	—	28	26	28	24
Our system of government and how well it works																
Optimistic	55	45	57	47	49	51	51	67	51	50	53	56	41	36	43	40
Pessimistic	15	24	14	21	22	21	21	28	21	23	43	38	33	38	28	34
Uncertain	27	29	26	29	26	26	27	—	24	25	—	—	23	23	28	25
Soundness of our free enterprise system over the long run																
Optimistic								67	—	—	57	61				
Pessimistic								24	—	—	34	28				
Uncertain								—	—	—	—	—				
Way our leaders are chosen under our political system																
Optimistic	46	45	55	44	52	56	57	—	55	50	—	—	49	49	50	47
Pessimistic	23	28	19	25	20	21	21	—	23	25	—	—	28	32	28	31
Uncertain	27	24	22	27	24	21	20	—	18	22	—	—	20	16	21	20

a. Question wording did not include the response of "uncertain."

Sources: Surveys by Roper Starch Worldwide (1974–1995, 1997) and the Gallup Organization (1996).

TABLE 2–4: CONFIDENCE IN DIFFERENT ASPECTS OF OUR LIVES IN THE FUTURE, 1973–1995
(percent)

QUESTION: Now, taking some specific aspects of our life, we'd like to know how confident you feel about them. Do you feel very confident, only fairly confident, or not at all confident that . . . ?

	Oct. 1973	*Oct. 1974*	*Oct. 1975*	*Oct. 1976*	*Sept. 1979*	*Sept. 1982*	*Sept. 1983*	*Sept. 1988*	*Sept. 1992*	*Sept. 1995*
This nation will continue to be a leader in world affairs										
Very confident	40	47	48	46	40	42	49	40	34	39
Only fairly confident	39	36	35	37	42	42	35	43	47	45
Not at all confident	14	12	13	13	15	12	13	11	14	13
Our free enterprise system will continue to work and keep this nation prosperous										
Very confident	34	38	35	41	36	34	42	38	31	33
Only fairly confident	45	45	47	43	48	51	43	47	52	52
Not at all confident	12	10	13	11	11	11	11	8	12	12
Our political system and method of selecting government leaders will continue to work										
Very confident					34	32	40	39	28	22
Only fairly confident					47	49	42	46	49	55
Not at all confident					13	15	13	9	16	19
Our system of checks and balances on the powers of the presidency, the Congress and the Supreme Court will continue to work										
Very confident	28	35	31	34	28	29	32	33	23	21
Only fairly confident	45	44	47	47	50	50	46	48	51	55
Not at all confident	14	11	15	12	13	13	14	10	19	18

NOTE: Not all categories shown.
SOURCE: Surveys by Roper Starch Worldwide, latest that of September 1995.

TABLE 2–5
IS THE GREAT AGE OF EXPANSION AND OPPORTUNITY OVER? 1939, 1990, AND1993
(percent)

QUESTION: Do you believe that the great age of economic expansion and opportunity in the United States is over, or that American industry can create a comparable expansion and opportunity in the future?

	Expansion Is Over	*Can Create a Comparable Expansion*
1939	13	72
1990	21	61
1993	20	57

SOURCES: Surveys by Elmo Roper for *Fortune* (1939) and Roper Starch Worldwide (1990, 1993).

TABLE 2–6
THE "CAN DO" SPIRIT, 1987–1997
(percent)

QUESTION: For each statement, please tell me if you completely agree with it, mostly agree with it, mostly disagree with it, or completely disagree with it . . . As Americans we can always find a way to solve our problems and get what we want.

	Completely Agree	*Mostly Agree*	*Mostly Disagree*	*Completely Disagree*
1987	12	56	24	4
1988	15	51	23	7
1989	14	55	23	5
1990	13	52	24	6
1991	19	49	22	8
1992	16	50	24	8
1993	12	47	31	7
1994	20	48	24	6
1997	19	52	20	7

SOURCE: Surveys by the Times Mirror/Pew Research Center for the People & the Press, latest that of November 1997.

TABLE 2–7
WOULD YOU LIKE TO SETTLE IN ANOTHER COUNTRY? 1948–1995
(percent)

QUESTION: If you were free to do so, would you like to go and settle in another country?
QUESTION: Please tell me whether you strongly agree, somewhat agree, somewhat disagree, or strongly disagree with the following statement . . . If I were free to do so, I would like to go and settle in another country.

	Yes/Agree	*No/Disagree*
Mar. 1948	3	93
Mar. 1949	6	93
Feb. 1950	5	93
Jan. 1960	6	91
Feb. 1971	11	86
Apr. 1972	13	87
Dec. 1972	11	86
Jan. 1974	10	87
June 1976	9	89
May 1991	9	90
Aug. 1994	19	79
Apr. 1995	12	87

SOURCES: Surveys by the Gallup Organization (1948–1991, 1995) and Luntz Research Companies (1994).

TABLE 2–8
PROUD TO BE AN AMERICAN? 1981–1995
(percent)

QUESTION: How proud are you to be an American?

	Very/Quite Proud	*Not Very/Not at All Proud*
June 1981	97	3
Dec. 1981	96	3
June 1986	99	1
June 1990	97	2
May 1991	96	3

QUESTION: How proud are you to be an American?

	Extremely/ Very Proud	*Somewhat/Not Very Proud*
Jan. 1989	94	7
May 1994	86	14

QUESTION: How proud are you of being an American citizen?

	Very/Somewhat Proud	*Not Very/Not at All Proud*
May 1995	96	3

SOURCES: For first panel, surveys by the Gallup Organization, latest that of May 1991. For second panel, surveys by the University of Michigan National Election Studies (1989) and the National Opinion Research Center (1994). For third panel, survey by CBS News.

TABLE 2–9
LEVEL OF PERSONAL FREEDOM IN THE UNITED STATES AND FIVE OTHER COUNTRIES, 1995
(percent)

QUESTION: Just your opinion, how far up or down on a 10-point scale would you rate each of the following nations in terms of the individual freedom granted to its citizens? A 10 means the highest level of personal freedom and a 1, the lowest. You can choose any number from 1 to 10.

	High (10–9–8)	*Average (7–6–5–4)*	*Low (3–2–1)*
United States	74	24	2
Canada	63	30	2
Great Britain	46	42	5
Mexico	7	63	24
Russia	4	52	39
China	4	34	56

SOURCE: Survey by the Gallup Organization, August 1995.

TABLE 2–10
THE UNITED STATES HAS THE BEST SYSTEM OF GOVERNMENT IN THE WORLD, 1992, 1994, AND 1996
(percent)

QUESTION: I'm going to read a few statements; for each, please tell me if you agree or disagree with it . . . Whatever its faults, the United States still has the best system of government in the world.

	Agree	*Disagree*
1992	85	14
1994	84	12
1996	83	15

SOURCE: Surveys by ABC News, latest that of May 1996.

TABLE 2–11
IS THE UNITED STATES THE GREATEST COUNTRY? 1955–1997
(percent)

QUESTION: Suppose you were talking to a person, in a general way, about the United States and other countries. Which one of these statements best expresses your own point of view?

A. The United States is the greatest country in the world, better than all other countries in every possible way.
B. The United States is a great country, but so are certain other countries.
C. In many respects, certain other countries are better than the United States.

	Greatest	*Great*	*Others Better*
1955	66	3	1
1991	37	54	9
1996[a]	55	41	4
1996	37	49	12

QUESTION: The United States is the greatest nation on earth.

	True	*False*
1997	83	13

QUESTION: To begin, we'd like your opinion of the United States compared to other countries . . . . Do you think the United States is the single best place in the world to live or one of several countries that are the best places in the world to live or not one of the best places in the world to live?

	Single Best	*One of Several Best Places*	*Not One of the Best*
1997	64	32	2

(Table continues)

TABLE 2–11 (continued)

QUESTION: Which of the following statements do you think best describes America's economic position?
A. America is the number-one economic power in the world today.
B. America is one of a few, about equal, economic powers.
C. America is a major economic power but not one of the leaders.
D. America is no longer a major economic power.

	Number One	*One of a Few*	*Major, but Not One of Leaders*	*No Longer a Power*
Jan. 1990	15	37	34	11
Jan. 1992	17	37	32	11
Mar. 1992	18	36	32	12
June 1997	36	33	23	6

a. Question wording varied slightly. It did not include the preface "Suppose you were talking . . . point of view." It asked: "Do you think the United States is the greatest country in the world, better than all others, the United States is a great country but so are certain other countries, or that there are some other countries better than the United States?"

SOURCES: For first panel, surveys by the Gallup Organization (1955–1996) and ABC News (1996). For second panel, survey by Princeton Survey Research Associates for Wisconsin Public Television, August 1997. For third panel, survey by Opinion Research Corporation International for *USA Weekend*, May 1997. For fourth panel, surveys by NBC News/*Wall Street Journal*, latest that of June 1997.

TABLE 2–12
America in Decline, 1990–1996
(percent)

Question: Do you think America is in a state of decline, or do you feel that this is not the case?

	Is in a State of Decline	*Is Not in a State of Decline*
Oct. 1990[a]	31	63
Oct. 1991	53	42
Dec. 1991	63	32
Jan. 1992	63	31
Feb. 1992	66	30
Jan. 1994	49	44
June 1994	51	44

Question: In general, do you think the United States is in decline as a nation, are we holding steady, or is the nation improving?

	In a State of Decline	*Holding Steady*	*Improving*
1996	52	40	9

Note: 1990–1992 samples are registered voters.
a. Question asked if America was in a *permanent* state of decline.
Sources: For first panel, surveys by NBC News/*Wall Street Journal*, latest that of June 1994. For second panel, survey by the Gallup Organization, April 1996.

TABLE 2–13
SATISFACTION WITH DEMOCRACY, 1991–1995
(percent)

QUESTION: In general, are you satisfied or dissatisfied with the way democracy is working in this country?

	Satisfied	*Dissatisfied*
May 1991	60	36
Jan. 1992	48	48
June 1992[a]	36	60
Oct. 1994	50	48
Aug. 1995	46	50

a. Registered voters.
SOURCE: Surveys by the Gallup Organization, latest that of August 1995.

TABLE 2–14
THE UNITED STATES IN THE FUTURE, 1992–1997
(percent)

QUESTION: Thinking about the future, would you say the United States is on the right track or the wrong track for the twenty-first century?

	Right Track	*Wrong Track*
1996	50	41

QUESTION: Now thinking ahead to the year 2000, do you think the United States will be in better shape than it is today, in worse shape, or about the same?

	Better	*Worse*	*Same*
1992	30	33	30
1996	31	31	31
1997	23	25	50

SOURCES: For first panel, survey by the Gallup Organization, September 1996. For second panel, surveys by Yankelovich Partners (1992) and the Gallup Organization (1996–1997).

TABLE 2–15
NATIONAL SPIRIT, 1981–1997
(percent)

QUESTION: Some people think that the United States will never again have it as good as we did in the past; others disagree. How about you? Do you think the country has already seen the best times we are going to, or not?

	Poll	*Already Seen Best Times*	*Has Not Yet Seen Best Times*
Mar. 1981	Civic Services	38	62
Nov. 1981	RSW	40	49
Aug. 1994	Roper/U. Conn.	43	50

QUESTION: Some people think that Americans will never be as well off again as they have been in the past. Others disagree and say that over the long run our standard of living will continue to go up. Do you think we have already seen our best days, or do you think things will get better?

	Already Seen Best Times	*Things Will Get Better*
1983[a]	34	62
1986	36	58
1988	30	61

QUESTION: I believe greatest days are ahead of the United States.

	True	*False*
1997	56	37

a. *New York Times* only.

SOURCES: For first panel, surveys by Civic Services Inc., Roper Starch Worldwide, and the Roper Center for Public Opinion Research/University of Connecticut for *Reader's Digest.* For second panel, surveys by CBS News/*New York Times*, latest that of September 1988. For third panel, survey by Opinion Research Corporation International for *USA Weekend*, May 1997.

TABLE 2–16
THE NOSTALGIA IMPULSE, 1937–1997
(percent)

QUESTION: Do you think Americans were happier and more contented at that time [during the horse-and-buggy days] than they are now?
QUESTION: We hear people talk about the "good old days." Do you think the "good old days" were better than the present or not?

	Yes	*No*
1939	62	26
1994	56	32

QUESTION: Do you think religion is gaining or losing influence in the life of the nation?
QUESTION: At the present time, do you think religion as a whole is increasing its influence on American life, or losing its influence?

	Gaining Influence	*Losing Influence*
1937[a]	25	50
1997	36	60

QUESTION: Do you think that sexual moral standards in this country are better or worse than they were a generation ago?
QUESTION: In the past 20 years or so, do you think there has been a severe breakdown in moral standards in America, or don't you think so?
QUESTION: Generally speaking, do you think moral values have become stronger in the United States in the last 25 years, do you think they have become weaker, or do you think they have stayed about the same?

	Poll	*Are Better/ Stronger*	*Are Worse/ Weaker*	*Same*
1937	*Fortune*	17	45	28[b]
1988	CBS/*NYT*	22	72	—
1996	Gallup	7	76	16

a. Had a "same" category of 17 percent.
b. Volunteered response.
SOURCES: For first panel, surveys by the Gallup Organization (1939) and Roper Starch Worldwide (1994). For second panel, surveys by Elmo Roper for *Fortune* (1937) and the Gallup Organization (1997). For third panel, surveys by Elmo Roper for *Fortune*, CBS News/*New York Times*, and the Gallup Organization.

CHAPTER 3

Sense of Self, Sense of Nation

Sense of Self

Survey questions generally show high satisfaction and happiness with personal life. We display here two questions asked over a long time span. For half a century, only a small minority (around 10 percent) have described their lives as "not too happy." Huge majorities have told Gallup since 1979 that they are satisfied with their personal lives (table 3–1). A question Gallup began asking in 1948 delves into specific aspects of personal life. It shows very high satisfaction with housing, jobs, standard of living, and even household income (table 3–2). Over 80 percent told Harris in early 1997 that they felt good about their relations with their families, their homes, the quality of their life overall, their health, their social life, and their standard of living (table 3–3). More than 80 percent in 1983, 1994, and 1996 said they were optimistic about their personal futures (table 3–4). Seventy-six percent in 1975 and 72 percent twenty-one years later in 1996 thought their chances of achieving the "good life" were very or fairly good. Only 5 percent or less in eight iterations of this question between 1975 and 1996 said their chances were not good at all (table 3–5). Tables 3–6 and 3–7 also show more optimism than pessimism about people's standard of living compared with the past and looking ahead to the future.

In 1959, Lloyd Free and Albert Cantril developed a statistical measure in which respondents are asked to think about the rungs on a ladder, with the top rung representing the best possible life and the lowest rung, the worst possible. Those interviewed are asked where they put themselves on the ladder today, where they were five years ago, and where they think they will be five years from now (tables 3–8 and 3–9). In our forward-looking country, in only two instances (1980 and 1982) were people more satisfied with the past than the present. In every instance, people were more optimistic about where they would be in the future than satisfied with their current positions.

Other questions in this overview of how we think we are doing personally tap more specific concerns. Since 1974, strong pluralities have told Roper Starch Worldwide that their families are getting along only fairly well. Usually about 20 percent or more give the most optimistic response and say they are getting along quite well. About a quarter indicate that they feel quite pinched, and fewer than 10 percent give the most pessimistic response, that they are not making ends meet (table 3–10). Another question asked since 1975 finds huge majorities saying that it is unlikely that they will lose their job in the next year (table 3–11). Majorities in table 3–12 say they do not now earn enough money to lead the kind of life they want, but most people in this group expect they will in the future. Table 3–13 shows optimism outweighing pessimism about the quality of life in this country and the institution of marriage and family, although in both cases the number feeling pessimistic has risen.

One of the most consistent findings in survey research involves optimism about personal life side by side with pessimism about the larger society. As a bridge to the next section that examines our perceptions of how the nation is doing, we have included here a series of questions that highlight this discrepancy (table 3–14). People are much more satisfied with their doctor than they are with the medical profession. They are more satisfied with their schools than with schools in the nation. They think their own representative in Congress deserves reelection; they do not feel that way about most members. Perhaps surprisingly, given all the jokes about lawyers and stock brokers, people are quite positive about the lawyers and the brokers they have used, and they are more positive about them than they are about those professions as a whole. Americans feel fairly good about the morals and values of people in their community but not about the morals and values of Americans in general. A divergence of opinion appears on the state of race relations, too. In a June 1997 CBS News poll, 72 percent said race relations in their community are generally good; 38 percent feel that way about race relations in the country. Optimism or satisfaction declines as one moves from things that are closest to people (their families, or their local communities) to those that are remote (table 3–15).

Sense of Nation

We begin now to look at people's sense of how things are going in the country. Table 3–16 contrasts satisfaction with the way things are going in people's personal lives and satisfaction with the way things are going in the United States. The pictures are quite different. During 1979, an average of 76 percent were satisfied with their personal lives, and an average of only 19 percent were satisfied with the way things were going in the nation (a fifty-seven-percentage point difference). In February 1997, 85 percent were satisfied with their personal lives; in late February 1998, when the question was asked about the way things are going in the United States, 64 percent were satisfied (table 3–16). The public is more satisfied now than it was in the late 1970s.

Roper Starch Worldwide has found large majorities saying since 1971 that the current year has been very or fairly good for them. When asked about the next year for themselves and then separately for the country, people are consistently more optimistic about their personal future than they are about the nation's future (table 3–17).

The ladder ratings about the country provide a different impression from those about people's personal lives. People are usually more content about where they are today than with their position on the ladder five years earlier. That is not the case for perceptions of the country. On a number of occasions, people thought the country's past was better than its present (tables 3–18 and 3–19). Still, in nearly every asking of this question, confidence about where the country will be five years from now is higher than confidence about where it is today.

Whether things in the country are going in the right direction or have gotten "pretty seriously off on the wrong track" is one of the most popular questions in the survey business. The question has been asked scores of times by different survey organizations over the past quarter-century. Wirthlin Worldwide, for example, has asked the question about 250 times since 1975; ABC News and the *Washington Post,* more than 75 times since 1982; and Roper Starch Worldwide, nearly 50 times since 1973. (For space considerations, we have averaged the numbers for each survey organization for each year.) What tables 3–20a and 3–20b show is that there have been very few instances when a majority believed things in the country were going in the right direction. Majorities, usually large ones, say the country is on the wrong track (table 3–20 a, b).

Several pollsters have posed follow-up questions, asking people to explain in their own words why they give the responses they do. The evidence we have seen suggests that people think the country is on the wrong track because of worries about the country's moral fiber, not because of political concerns. A long battery of questions asked by Roper Starch Worldwide underscores this deep concern about the moral life of the nation (see table 3–13 for some of these questions). Table 3–13, for example, shows that 36 percent of those surveyed in 1974 were pessimistic about "moral and ethical standards in the country today" and 32 percent were optimistic. In March 1997, 51 percent were pessimistic, and 27 percent were optimistic. In 1997, there was only one other item in the list of twelve that Roper Starch Worldwide inquired about that produced a more pessimistic response: 64 percent were pessimistic about the amount of crime and violence in this country, and only 16 percent were optimistic.

Table 3–21 shows one side of the responses to two questions Yankelovich Partners has asked since the mid-1970s. The ups and downs on these two questions are a referendum on the way things are going in the country, as the misery index that accompanies the table shows. The misery index, popularized by Ronald Reagan in the 1980 presidential campaign, is the sum of the unemployment and inflation rates.

TABLE 3–1
SATISFACTION AND HAPPINESS WITH THE WAY THINGS ARE GOING, 1947–1997
(percent)

QUESTION: In general, are you satisfied or dissatisfied with the way things are going in your own personal life?[a]
QUESTION: Taken all together, how would you say things are these days—would you say that you are very happy, pretty happy, or not too happy?[b]

	Satisfied	*Dissatisfied*	*Very Happy*	*Pretty Happy*	*Not Too Happy*
1947[c]	—	—	38	58	4
1957[d]	—	—	35	54	11
1979	76	21	—	—	—
1981	81	17	—	—	—
1982	75	23	35	54	12
1983	77	20	32	56	12
1984	79	18	36	52	12
1985	82	17	30	60	11
1986	84	15	33	57	10
1987	83	15	34	55	12
1988	85	13	36	56	8
1989	—	—	35	57	9
1990	84	14	36	57	8
1991	83	15	33	58	10
1992	78	21	—	—	—
1993	82	17	33	57	10
1994	—	—	31	58	11
1995[c]	83	11	—	—	—
1996	86	12	30	57	12
1997	85	14	—	—	—

a. Numbers from each year are the average for the year or, if only one point is available, that point is used.
b. We have omitted data on the happiness question between 1957 and 1982 to make the table easier to read. The responses are similar to the ones shown above.
c. Question wording varies slightly.
d. University of Michigan.
SOURCES: Surveys by the Gallup Organization, the University of Michigan's Survey Research Center, and the National Opinion Research Center.

TABLE 3–2
PERCENTAGE SATISFIED WITH VARIOUS ASPECTS OF LIFE, 1948–1997
(percent)

QUESTION: Please tell me whether you are generally satisfied or dissatisfied with each of the following: your housing situation; your job, or the work you do; the future facing you and your family; your standard of living—that is, the things you can buy or do; your family or household income.

	Housing	*Job*	*Future*	*Standard of Living*	*Household Income*
Dec. 1948	69				
July 1963	72	85	64	77	64
Aug. 1965	72	—	—	—	65
Sept. 1965	71	82	71	—	65
Sept. 1966	78	—	—	—	66
Oct. 1966	79	—	63	—	65
Nov. 1966	75	86	—	—	65
Feb. 1968	—	—	55	—	—
Apr. 1969	76	—	—	—	64
Apr. 1969	78	87	—	—	66
Aug. 1971	75	—	55	—	63
Aug. 1971	—	—	43	—	—
Dec. 1971	74	84	58	78	63
Sept. 1973	74	79	53	71	61
Dec. 1974	76	75	—	71	—
Jan. 1977	—	—	64	—	—
June 1977	—	—	47	—	—
July 1977	—	—	64	—	—
Nov. 1977	77	—	—	71	65
Sept. 1978	—	—	41	—	—
Dec. 1981	86	82	—	82	69
Dec. 1984	82	70	—	76	58
Sept. 1988	87	76	—	85	69
Oct. 1988	87	76	—	85	69
Feb. 1991	—	—	80	—	—
Dec. 1991	85	71	71	70	65
June 1994	—	86	—	—	—
Apr. 1995	90	73	—	75	72
Feb. 1997	88	84	—	85	69
Aug. 1997	—	86	—	—	—

SOURCE: Surveys by the Gallup Organization, latest that of August 1997.

TABLE 3–3
WHAT PEOPLE FEEL GOOD ABOUT, 1997
(percent)

QUESTION: Next, we'd like to know whether or not you feel good about various things in this country and in your own life. Do you feel good about [read each item], or not?

	Feel Good About	*Do Not Feel Good About*
Your relations with your family	95	4
Your home	92	8
The quality of your life overall	91	8
Your health	88	12
Your social life	86	12
Your standard of living	83	16
The quality of the air, water, and environment where you live and work	61	38
Your marriage, if you are married	60	4
Your job, if you have one	60	15
Your financial security for the future	55	43
Your children's future	48	31

NOTE: Some additional responses to this question are on tables 3–14 and 3–15.
SOURCE: Survey by Louis Harris and Associates, April 1997.

TABLE 3–4
OPTIMISM OR PESSIMISM ABOUT YOUR OWN FUTURE, 1983, 1994, AND 1996
(percent)

QUESTION: Would you say you are optimistic or pessimistic about your own personal future?
QUESTION: Please tell me whether you strongly agree, somewhat agree, somewhat disagree or strongly disagree with the following statement . . . I am optimistic about my personal future.

	Optimistic/Agree	*Pessimistic/Disagree*
Dec. 1983	82	13
Aug. 1994	81	17
May 1996	89	8
Nov. 1996	80	16

SOURCES: Surveys by ABC News (1983, May 1996) and Luntz Research Companies (1994, Nov. 1996).

TABLE 3–5

CHANCES OF ACHIEVING THE GOOD LIFE, SELECTED YEARS, 1975–1996
(percent)

QUESTION: Thinking of your concept of the good life, how good do you think your chances are of achieving it—very good, fairly good, not very good, or not good at all?

	Very Good	*Fairly Good*	*Not Very Good*	*Not Good at All*	*Already Achieved It*[a]
1975	35	41	10	4	9
1978	35	40	10	4	9
1981	32	42	8	5	9
1984	35	41	9	4	9
1988	28	45	11	5	7
1991	23	46	15	5	6
1994	20	47	16	5	10
1996	24	48	14	5	6

a. Volunteered response.
SOURCE: Surveys by Roper Starch Worldwide, latest that of December 1996.

TABLE 3–6

YOUR STANDARD OF LIVING COMPARED WITH PAST FIVE YEARS, 1978 AND 1995
(percent)

QUESTION: Do you personally feel that your standard of living over the past 5 years has improved, declined, or what?

	Improved	*Declined*	*Stayed the Same*[a]
1978	45	19	34
1995	56	17	26

a. Volunteered response.
SOURCE: Surveys by Cambridge Reports/Research International, latest that of January 1995.

TABLE 3–7
YOUR STANDARD OF LIVING IN THE NEXT FIVE YEARS, 1978–1995
(percent)

QUESTION: Over the next 5 years do you think your standard of living will improve, decline, or what?

	Will Improve	*Decline*	*Stay the Same*[a]
1978	46	13	30
1989	46	14	33
1992	53	15	28
1993	58	12	26
1994	54	16	25
1995	54	12	28

a. Volunteered response.
SOURCE: Surveys by Cambridge Reports/Research International, latest that of January 1995.

TABLE 3–8
LADDER OF LIFE—YOUR LIFE, 1959–1998
(mean)

QUESTION: Here is a ladder scale. It represents the "ladder of life." As you see, it is a ladder with 11 rungs numbered 0 to 10. Let's suppose the top of the ladder represents the best possible life for you as you describe it, and the bottom rung represents the worst possible life for you as you describe it. On which rung of the ladder do you feel your life is today?
QUESTION: On which rung do you think you were 5 years ago?
QUESTION: On which rung do you think you will be 5 years from now?

	Poll	*5 Years Ago*	*Today*	*5 Years from Now*
1959	Gallup	5.9	6.6	7.8
1964	Gallup	6.0	6.9	7.9
1971	Gallup	5.8	6.6	7.5
1972	Gallup	5.5	6.4	7.6
1974	Gallup	5.5	6.6	7.4
1974	Cambridge	6.1	6.3	7.0

(Table continues)

TABLE 3–8 (continued)

	Poll	*5 Years Ago*	*Today*	*5 Years from Now*
1975	Gallup	5.5	6.1	6.7
1975	Cambridge	5.9	6.2	6.9
1976	Gallup	5.7	6.7	7.7
1976	Cambridge	5.7	6.1	7.0
1977	Cambridge	5.6	6.2	7.1
1978	Cambridge	6.0	6.4	6.8
1979	Gallup	5.8	6.4	7.0
1979	Cambridge	6.2	6.6	7.3
1980	Cambridge	6.3	6.2	7.0
1981	Gallup	6.0	6.4	7.3
1982	Gallup	5.9	6.3	6.5
1982	Cambridge	6.4	6.3	7.2
1983	Cambridge	6.3	6.6	7.5
1984	Cambridge	6.2	6.9	8.5
1985	Gallup	5.8	6.4	7.6
1985	Cambridge	5.8	6.3	7.5
1986	Cambridge	5.9	6.3	7.5
1987	Gallup	5.8	6.5	7.7
1987	Cambridge	5.7	6.3	7.4
1988	Cambridge	5.8	6.2	7.1
1989	Gallup	6.0	6.4	7.4
1989	Cambridge	4.9	5.4	6.7
1996	Pew	5.8	6.7	7.7
1997	Pew	5.9	7.0	8.2
1998	Pew	5.9	7.1	8.2

NOTE: Between 1974 and 1980, fourth-quarter Cambridge numbers are used. In other years, Cambridge asked the question only once.

SOURCES: Surveys by the Institute for International Social Research, the Gallup Organization, Cambridge Reports/Research International, and the Pew Research Center for the People & the Press.

TABLE 3–9
Ladder of Life—Your Life, 1985–1995
(mean)

Question: Let's talk about the quality of your life. Please imagine a ladder with 10 steps representing the "ladder of life." Let's suppose the top of the ladder, the 10th step, represents the best possible life for you; and the bottom, the 1st step, the worst possible life for you. On which step of the ladder do you personally stand at the present time?
Question: On which step would you say you stood 5 years ago?
Question: Just as your best guess, on which will you stand in the future, say about 5 years from now?

	5 Years Ago	*Today*	*5 Years from Now*
1985	5.7	6.2	7.3
1986	5.4	6.1	7.3
1988	5.5	6.6	8.1
1991	5.5	6.2	7.5
1992[a]	5.7	6.2	7.8
1994	5.6	6.4	7.7
1995	5.5	6.5	7.7

Note: Question was asked only once each year except in 1992 when it was asked five times.
a. Numbers from December survey.
Source: Surveys by Wirthlin Worldwide, latest that of April 1995.

TABLE 3–10
HOW YOUR FAMILY IS MAKING OUT, 1974–1995
(percent)

QUESTION: Considering your income and what you have to live on and the cost of living, how would you say your family is making out today—all things considered, would you say you are getting along all right, or getting along only fairly well, or feeling quite pinched, or just not able to make ends meet?

	All Right	*Fairly Well*	*Quite Pinched*	*Not Making Ends Meet*
Nov. 1974	25	41	28	6
Feb. 1975	24	40	27	9
Apr. 1975	32	39	22	7
May 1975	27	38	25	9
June 1975	28	41	25	6
Nov. 1975	27	39	26	7
Jan. 1976	27	42	24	6
June 1976	28	41	23	6
Jan. 1977	32	41	20	7
June 1977	29	41	23	7
Jan. 1978	30	42	21	7
June 1978	24	40	27	8
Nov. 1978	23	41	28	8
Jan. 1979	24	42	27	6
June 1979	24	37	30	9
Nov. 1979	22	39	31	9
Mar. 1991	26	40	27	6
Dec. 1995	20	48	25	6

SOURCE: Surveys by Roper Starch Worldwide, latest that of December 1995.

TABLE 3–11
LIKELY THAT YOU WILL LOSE YOUR JOB? 1975–1997
(percent)

QUESTION: Thinking about the next 12 months, how likely do you think it is that you will lose your job or be laid off—is it very likely, fairly likely, not too likely, or not at all likely?

	Poll	*Likely*	*Unlikely*
Jan. 1975	Gallup	15	81
Apr. 1975	Gallup	12	85
Oct. 1976	Gallup	12	85
1977	NORC	10	89
1978	NORC	7	93
Nov. 1979	Gallup	11	84
May 1980	Gallup	14	84
Sept. 1980	Gallup	15	84
1982	NORC	13	87
Jan. 1982	Gallup	15	82
May 1982	ABC/*WP*	23	75
June 1982	Gallup	15	81
June 1982	ABC	24	75
Aug. 1982	*LAT*	19	77
Nov. 1982	Gallup	19	77
Nov. 1982	*LAT*	19	79
1983	NORC	14	86
Apr. 1983	Gallup	16	81
Apr. 1983	*LAT*	16	83
Dec. 1984[a]	Black	23	73
1985	NORC	11	89
1986	NORC	11	90
Feb. 1987	ABC/*Money*	19	79
Oct. 1987	ABC	19	81
1988	NORC	9	91
1989	NORC	8	92
Feb. 1989	Gallup	12	88
Dec. 1989	*LAT*	12	82
1990	NORC	8	92
Mar. 1990	ABC/*Money*	16	82

(Table continues)

TABLE 3–11 (continued)

	Poll	*Likely*	*Unlikely*
July 1990	Gallup	12	86
Oct. 1990	Gallup	16	83
Dec. 1990	ABC/*Money*	13	86
1991	NORC	13	87
Mar. 1991	Gallup	12	87
June 1991	ABC/*WP*	19	80
July 1991	Gallup	15	84
Oct. 1991	ABC/*WP*	15	83
Oct. 1991	ABC/*WP*	18	81
Oct. 1991	Gallup	14	85
Nov. 1991	ABC/*Money*	19	81
Dec. 1991	ABC/*WP*	22	78
Feb. 1992	ABC/*WP*	19	80
Mar. 1992	ABC/*Money*	17	81
1993	NORC	12	88
June 1993	ABC/*Money*	21	78
June 1993	PSRA	15	83
Sept. 1993[a]	*LAT*	29	67
Dec. 1993	Gallup	12	86
1994	NORC	10	90
Oct. 1995[a]	*LAT*	30	68
1996	NORC	11	88
Mar. 1996	ABC/*WP*	22	76
Apr. 1996	Gallup	14	85
Dec. 1996	*NYT*	13	85
May 1997	ABC/*Money*	13	86
June 1997	Gallup	9	89
Oct. 1997	ABC	13	86

NOTE: Responses combined. Question wording varies slightly.
a. Question asks how likely you *or someone in your household* will lose a job.
SOURCES: Surveys by the Gallup Organization, National Opinion Research Center, ABC News/*Washington Post*, the *Los Angeles Times*, Gordon Black, ABC News/*Money*, Princeton Survey Research Associates, and the *New York Times*.

TABLE 3–12
EARN ENOUGH MONEY? 1992–1997
(percent)

QUESTION: Do you now earn enough money to lead the kind of life you want, or not?
QUESTION: [To those who answered no] Do you think you will be able to earn enough money in the future to lead the kind of life you want, or not?

	Poll	*Yes*	*No*
	Employed people's response[a]		
Jan. 1992	*US News*	39	61
May 1992	*US News*	34	65
Aug. 1992	*US News*	33	66
Oct. 1992	*US News*	36	63
Mar. 1994	Times Mirror	44	56
Feb. 1995	Times Mirror	41	58
June 1996	Pew	44	56
Sept. 1996[b]	Pew	44	55
May 1997	Pew	46	54
Nov. 1997	Pew	41	59
	Employed respondents who answered no[c]		
Jan. 1992	*US News*	34	22
May 1992	*US News*	34	28
Aug. 1992	*US News*	36	25
Oct. 1992	*US News*	35	23
Mar. 1994	Times Mirror	33	20
Feb. 1995	Times Mirror	35	20
June 1996	Pew	34	20
Sept. 1996[b]	Pew	33	18
May 1997	Pew	34	18
Nov. 1997	Pew	33	24

a. Currently earning enough money.
b. Registered voters.
c. Will earn enough money in the future.
SOURCES: Surveys by Princeton Survey Research Associates for *U.S. News & World Report* and Times Mirror/Pew Research Center for the People & the Press.

TABLE 3–13

OPTIMISTIC OR PESSIMISTIC ABOUT DIFFERENT ASPECTS OF LIFE IN THE FUTURE, 1974–1997

(percent)

QUESTION: As I read a list of items, please say whether you feel generally optimistic about it as far as the future is concerned, generally pessimistic about it, or uncertain about it.

	Aug. 1974	*Aug. 1975*	*Feb. 1977*	*Aug. 1977*	*Feb. 1979*	*Feb. 1981*	*Feb. 1983*	*Oct. 1986*[a]	*Feb. 1988*	*Feb. 1991*	*Jan. 1992*[a]	*Jan. 1993*[a]	*Feb. 1994*	*Feb. 1995*	*Mar. 1996*	*Mar. 1997*
Quality of life in this country																
Optimistic	59	61	62	60	57	63	65	73	64	58	59	66	53	48	59	53
Pessimistic	17	17	16	18	17	17	16	23	17	21	38	31	25	31	21	28
Uncertain	21	19	20	20	23	19	17	—	17	18	—	—	20	19	19	17
Institution of marriage and the family																
Optimistic	57	57	48	52	55	56	58	—	57	62	—	—	50	41	54	49
Pessimistic	19	20	27	25	22	23	20	—	25	19	—	—	29	40	27	31
Uncertain	19	20	22	20	20	19	20	—	15	17	—	—	18	17	17	18
Opportunities for you to get ahead																
Optimistic								70	—	—	57	60				
Pessimistic								22	—	—	35	31				
Uncertain								—	—	—	—	—				
Moral and ethical standards in our country																
Optimistic	32	31	29	26	26	30	33	—	31	35	—	—	27	19	24	27
Pessimistic	36	39	39	43	43	44	40	—	44	37	—	—	50	61	53	51
Uncertain	28	26	29	28	27	25	25	—	22	25	—	—	20	18	21	20

a. Question wording did not include the response of "uncertain."

SOURCES: Surveys by Roper Starch Worldwide (1974–1995, 1997) and the Gallup Organization (1996).

TABLE 3–14
PERSONAL ASSOCIATIONS, NATIONAL ONES, 1993–1997
(percent)

QUESTION: How would you rate the honesty and ethical standards of people in these different fields—very high, high, average, low, or very low [lawyers, medical doctors]?

	Own Lawyer	*Lawyers*
Very high, high	50	16
Average	22	40
Very low, low	7	41
	Own Doctor[a]	*Doctors*
Very high, high	78	51
Average	11	37
Very low, low	7	11

QUESTION: What grade would you give the public schools in [this community/the nation as a whole]?

	Schools Locally	*Schools Nationally*
A	9	1
B	30	17
C	33	48
D	14	22
F	9	6

QUESTION: Would you like to see your representative in Congress be reelected in the next congressional election, or not?
QUESTION: Regardless of how you feel about your own representative, would you like to see most members of Congress reelected in the next congressional election, or not?

	Own Representative	*Most Members*
Yes	66	44
No	23	43

(Table continues)

TABLE 3–14 (continued)

QUESTION: How much of the time do you trust [local government/state government/government in Washington] to do what is right—would you say just about always, most of the time, or only some of the time?

	Local Government	*State Government*	*Federal Government*
Just about always	10	9	5
Most of the time	47	45	29
Some of the time	40	43	62
None of the time[b]	2	3	4

QUESTION: Please tell me whether you strongly agree with the statement, somewhat agree, somewhat disagree, or strongly disagree . . . The advice I get from my broker helps me make smarter investment decisions . . . I have a lot of trust in brokers and brokerage firms.

	Own Broker	*Most Brokers*
Strongly/somewhat agree	74	49

QUESTION: Next, we'd like to know whether or not you feel good about various things in this country and in your own life. Do you feel good about [read each item], or not?[c]

	Feel Good About	*Do Not Feel Good About*
The morals and values of people in your community	65	33
The morals and values of Americans in general	34	62

(Table continues)

TABLE 3–14 (continued)

QUESTION: Do you think race relations in your community are generally good or generally bad?
QUESTION: Do you think race relations in the United States are generally good or generally bad?

	Your Community	*United States*
Good	72	38
Bad	23	52

a. The question for "own doctor" is whether or not you have a favorable, neutral, or unfavorable opinion of your own doctor.
b. Volunteered response.
c. Some additional responses to this question are on tables 3–3 and 3–15.
SOURCES: For first panel (own lawyer/doctor), Peter D. Hart Research Associates, January 1993. For lawyers/doctors in general, survey by the Gallup Organization, July 1993. For second panel (schools), survey by NBC News/*Wall Street Journal*, March 1997. The third panel (congressional representatives), survey by the Pew Research Center for the People & the Press, January 1998. For fourth panel (government), survey by ABC News, May 1996. For fifth panel (brokers), survey by Yankelovich Partners, September 1995. For sixth panel (morals and values), survey by Louis Harris and Associates, April 1997. For seventh panel (race relations), survey by CBS News, June 1997.

TABLE 3–15
PERSONAL OPTIMISM, NATIONAL PESSIMISM, 1994 AND 1997
(percent)

QUESTION: All in all, are you satisfied or dissatisfied with the way things are going in [your personal life, your local community, this country today]?

	Satisfied	*Dissatisfied*
Personal life	83	14
Local community	68	27
This country	24	71

QUESTION: Would you say things in [your own life and that of your family, your local community, your state] are generally headed in the right direction or pretty seriously off on the wrong track?
QUESTION: Do you feel things in this country are generally going in the right direction today, or do you feel that things have pretty seriously gotten off on the wrong track?

	Right Direction	*Wrong Track*
You and your family	88	10
Local community	63	30
State	46	46
Country	26	62

QUESTION: Next, we'd like to know whether or not you feel good about various things in this country and in your own life. Do you feel good about [read each item], or not?[a]

	Feel Good About	*Do Not Feel Good About*
The city, town or county in which you live	79	20
The state of the nation	52	45

a. Some additional responses to this question are on tables 3–3 and 3–14.
SOURCES: For first panel, survey by the Times Mirror Center for the People & the Press, March 1994. For second panel, survey by Luntz Research Companies and Roper Starch Worldwide, August 1994. For third panel, survey by Louis Harris and Associates, April 1997.

TABLE 3–16
Satisfaction with the Way Things Are Going, Yearly Average, 1979–1998
(percent)

QUESTION: In general, are you satisfied or dissatisfied with the way things are going in your own personal life?
QUESTION: In general, are you satisfied or dissatisfied with the way things are going in the United States at this time?

	Personal Life[a]		*United States*[b]	
	Satisfied	Dissatisfied	Satisfied	Dissatisfied
1979	76	21	19	77
1981	81	17	26	69
1982	75	23	24	72
1983	77	20	35	59
1984	79	18	50	44
1985	82	17	51	46
1986	84	15	57	39
1987	83	15	45	49
1988	85	13	49	47
1989	—	—	45	50
1990	84	14	40	56
1991	83	15	49	47
1992	78	21	21	77
1993	82	17	28	69
1994	—	—	33	64
1995	83[c]	11[c]	32	65
1996	86	12	39	57
1997	85	14	49	48
1998	—	—	62	35

NOTE: Numbers from each year are the average for the year, or, if only one point is available, that point is used.
a. From 1979 to 1988 this question was asked three times or less each year. In 1990, it was asked nine times; 1991, eight; 1992, two; 1993, one; 1995, one; 1996, one; and 1997, one.
b. From 1979 to 1989 this question was asked three times or less each year. In 1990, it was asked nine times; 1991, twelve; 1992, ten; 1993, five; 1994, nine; 1995, three; 1996, nine; 1997, five times; and 1998, three times.
c. Question wording varies slightly.
SOURCE: Surveys by the Gallup Organization.

TABLE 3–17
Current Assessments and Expectations, 1971–1997
(percent)

QUESTION: [The current year] is drawing to a close. What kind of year has it been for you—very good, fairly good, not so good, or not at all good?
QUESTION: Do you expect [next year] to be a better year for you than [the current year], about the same, or not as good as [current year]?
QUESTION: Now, at the beginning of this interview I asked you what [next year] looked like to you in personal terms. Thinking about the country as a whole, what kind of year do you think [next year] will be for the nation—better than [the current year], about the same, or not as good as [the current year]?

	Current Year		*Expectation for Next Year* Personal			Country		
	Very/ fairly good	Not so good/not at all good	*Better*	*Same*	*Not as good*	*Better*	*Same*	*Not as good*
1971	79	20	46	41	7	38	41	12
1973	80	19	35	36	24	12	23	62
1974	74	25	34	39	23	16	27	51
1975	79	22	47	41	6	38	40	17
1976	78	21	52	37	6	47	40	10
1977	81	18	48	43	5	34	51	12
1978	81	19	46	39	12	23	42	31
1979	77	23	44	39	15	27	41	28
1980	76	24	46	37	10	38	40	16
1981	76	24	44	38	14	25	36	33
1982	70	28	46	42	8	37	42	17
1983	78	22	56	37	4	47	39	10
1984	80	20	50	40	8	34	52	12
1985	78	21	55	38	4	37	48	11
1986	81	19	53	39	5	30	49	18
1987	80	19	53	40	4	27	49	20
1988	78	21	53	38	5	29	57	10
1989	79	20	54	38	4	33	52	11

(Table continues)

TABLE 3–17 (continued)

	Current Year		*Expectation for Next Year*					
			Personal			Country		
	Very/ fairly good	Not so good/not at all good	*Better*	*Same*	*Not as good*	*Better*	*Same*	*Not as good*
1990	76	23	41	43	12	17	39	37
1991	67	32	40	47	9	25	47	21
1992	66	33	46	42	7	43	40	10
1993	71	29	51	36	8	35	45	15
1994	77	23	45	44	7	36	53	7
1995	74	16	47	43	7	—	—	—
1996	—	—	—	—	—	28	50	17
1996	79	21	51	40	5	32	54	10
1997	80	19	56	37	4	—	—	—

NOTE: All points shown above are from December except 1971 (October) and the first 1996 point (January).
SOURCE: Surveys by Roper Starch Worldwide, latest that of December 1997.

TABLE 3–18
LADDER OF LIFE, THE COUNTRY, 1959–1998
(mean)

QUESTION: Please look at this ladder again. The top rung represents the best possible state of affairs for the country as you describe it. The bottom rung represents the worst possible state of affairs for the country as you describe it. Now, I would like you to tell me on which rung you think the country is today; where it was 5 years ago; and where it will be 5 years from now.

	Poll	*5 Years Ago*	*Today*	*5 Years from Now*
1959	Gallup	6.5	6.7	7.4
1964	Gallup	6.1	6.5	7.7
1971	Gallup	6.2	5.4	6.2
1972	Gallup	5.6	5.5	6.2
1974	Gallup	6.3	4.8	5.8
1974	Cambridge	6.4	4.3	5.4
1975	Cambridge	5.8	4.6	5.4

(Table continues)

TABLE 3–18 (continued)

	Poll	*5 Years Ago*	*Today*	*5 Years from Now*
1976	Gallup	6.0	5.5	6.1
1976	Cambridge	5.1	4.9	6.0
1977	Cambridge	5.1	5.1	5.7
1978	Cambridge	5.7	4.9	5.0
1979	Cambridge	6.0	4.6	5.3
1980	Cambridge	6.1	4.4	5.7
1981	Gallup	6.0	5.1	6.3
1982	Gallup	6.5	5.3	6.0
1982	Cambridge	6.1	4.6	5.7
1983	Cambridge	5.6	5.1	6.2
1984	Cambridge	5.2	5.9	7.2
1985	Gallup	5.3	5.9	6.6
1985	Cambridge	5.0	5.3	6.0
1986	Cambridge	5.2	5.3	6.0
1987	Gallup	5.7	5.5	6.1
1987	Cambridge	5.5	5.3	5.9
1988	Cambridge	5.2	5.3	5.7
1989	Gallup	5.6	5.7	6.3
1989	Cambridge	4.6	4.3	5.1
1991	Gallup	5.6	5.7	5.6
1996	Pew	5.6	5.4	5.7
1997	Pew	5.7	5.6	5.9
1998	Pew	5.7	5.8	6.1

NOTE: Between 1974 and 1980, fourth-quarter Cambridge numbers are used. In other years, Cambridge asked the question only once.

SOURCES: Surveys by the Institute for International Social Research, the Gallup Organization, Cambridge Reports/Research International, and the Pew Research Center for the People & the Press.

TABLE 3–19
LADDER OF LIFE, UNITED STATES, 1979–1998
(mean)

QUESTION: I have some questions about how you'd rate the way things are going in the United States. On a scale of 1 to 10—if 1 were the *worst* possible situation, and 10 were the *best* possible situation—what number would you give to the way things are going at the present time?
QUESTION: Where would you say the United States was 5 years ago? Remember 1 is the worst possible situation, and 10 is the best possible situation.
QUESTION: And, just as your best guess, if things go pretty much as you now expect, how would you rate the United States 5 years from now?

	5 Years Ago	*Today*	*5 Years from Now*
1979	6.48	4.83	4.30
1981	5.68	5.19	5.72
1983[a]	5.71	5.52	6.04
1983[a]	5.48	5.58	6.13
1985	4.95	5.97	6.48
1988	5.80	5.73	5.84
1989	5.62	6.05	6.19
1990	6.25	4.91	4.96
1992	6.54	4.63	4.97
1993	6.16	5.20	5.75
1997	5.91	5.64	5.53
1998	5.85	5.84	6.11

a. *New York Times* only.
SOURCE: Surveys by CBS News/*New York Times*, latest that of January 1998.

TABLE 3–20a
THE RIGHT DIRECTION, YEARLY AVERAGE, 1973–1998
(percent)

QUESTION: Do you think things in this country are generally going in the right direction, or do you feel things have gotten pretty seriously off on the wrong track?

	RSW	*CBS/ NYT*	*WW*	*ABC/ WP*	*NBC/ WSJ*	*LAT*
1973	16					
1974	15					
1975	19		27			
1976	—		31			
1977	41		—			
1978	34		—			
1979	20		18			
1980	20		32			
1981	32		48			
1982	27		36	37		
1983	33	43	40	47		
1984	—	—	53	47		
1985	49	46	55	56		
1986	45	—	53	48		
1987	31	—	40	39		
1988	37	—	41	46		
1989	41	—	41	46	42	
1990	38	—	36	38	40	
1991	34	53	37	37	37	41
1992	23	—	20	20	20	20
1993	31	—	30	30	35	35
1994	29	30	28	28	32	29
1995	30	25	26	25	30	31
1996	31	41	31	35	35	35
1997	41	—	38	37	44	42
1998	—	51	—	53	50	53

NOTE: Numbers from each year are the average for the year, or, if only one point is available, that point is used; 1998 numbers are partial year only.
SOURCES: Surveys by Roper Starch Worldwide, CBS News/*New York Times*, Wirthlin Worldwide, ABC News/*Washington Post*, NBC News/*Wall Street Journal*, and the *Los Angeles Times*.

TABLE 3–20b
The Wrong Track, Yearly Average, 1973–1998
(percent)

Question: Do you think things in this country are generally going in the right direction, or do you feel things have gotten pretty seriously off on the wrong track?

	RSW	*CBS/ NYT*	*WW*	*ABC/ WP*	*NBC/ WSJ*	*LAT*
1973	74					
1974	75					
1975	71		65			
1976	—		64			
1977	44		—			
1978	53		—			
1979	65		77			
1980	70		55			
1981	54		45			
1982	63		58	57		
1983	58	49	54	49		
1984	—	—	42	48		
1985	39	44	43	40		
1986	42	—	45	48		
1987	57	—	56	57		
1988	49	—	51	47		
1989	44	—	50	51	35	
1990	51	—	55	59	40	
1991	55	37	55	58	46	49
1992	64	—	74	76	65	73
1993	55	—	61	66	45	54
1994	59	65	63	67	49	62
1995	56	64	65	71	50	59
1996	57	49	60	61	46	56
1997	47	—	53	60	40	49
1998	—	41	—	42	33	38

Note: Numbers from each year are the average for the year, or, if only one point is available, that point is used; 1998 numbers are partial year only.
Sources: Surveys by Roper Starch Worldwide, CBS News/*New York Times*, Wirthlin Worldwide, ABC News/*Washington Post*, NBC News/*Wall Street Journal*, and the *Los Angeles Times*.

TABLE 3–21
MOOD OF COUNTRY, YEARLY AVERAGE, 1974–1998
(percent)

QUESTION: How do you feel things are going in the country these days—very well, fairly well, pretty badly, or very badly?
QUESTION: In commenting on how things are going in the country, some people tell us that the problems we face are no worse than at any other time in recent years. Others say the country is really in deep and serious trouble today. Which comes closest to your own feelings—the fact that: Problems are no worse than at other times . . . The country is in deep and serious trouble?

	Very/Fairly Well[a]	*No Worse*[a]	*Misery Index*[b]
1974	30	32	17
1975	33	34	17
1976	54	50	13
1977	66	57	13
1978	52	50	14
1979	34	31	17
1980	27	22	21
1981	43	39	18
1982	38	39	16
1983	53	48	13
1984	72	60	12
1985	68	57	11
1986	65	—	9
1987	59	50	10
1988	66	51	10
1989	66	—	10
1990	53	—	11
1991	49	—	11
1992	33	—	10
1993	45	—	10
1994	49	—	9
1995	51	42	8
1996	60	47	8
1997	64	49	7
1998	72	54	NA

NA = not available.
a. Numbers from each year are the average for the year, or, if only one point is available, that point is used; 1998 numbers are partial year only.
b. Misery index is an aggregate of the unemployment rate (calculated as the employment status of the civilian population by the U.S. Bureau of Labor Statistics and *Employment and Earnings,* monthly), and the inflation rate (calculated as the percent change in the consumer price indexes by the Bureau of Labor Statistics, *Monthly Labor Review,* and *Handbook of Labor Statistics*).
SOURCE: Surveys by Yankelovich Partners.

CHAPTER 4
Opportunity

Surveys conducted over the past forty-five years show little change in the belief that opportunity is present for those who are willing to work hard (table 4–1). Today, about four in ten say that there are more opportunities for Americans now than in the past, and slightly more than two in ten say there are fewer (table 4–2). Survey after survey supports the belief that the opportunities available to this generation are better than those its parents had. In 1939, 61 percent of those surveyed said their opportunities to succeed were better than those their parents had. When Roper Starch Worldwide last repeated the question in 1993, a virtually identical 63 percent gave that response. In the five iterations of the question in the fifty-year-plus time span, about two in ten have said their opportunities to succeed are not as good as the ones their parents had (table 4–3).

Many survey organizations ask people to compare specific dimensions of their lives and their parents' lives. The surveys show that most people say they are better prepared to get ahead than their parents were, are better off financially, have a higher standard of living, and enjoy a better quality of life (tables 4–4, 4–5, 4–6, and 4–7).

The picture painted by the polls is fuzzier when people are asked about opportunities for children. Americans are not as optimistic about their children's prospects as their own prospects (compared with their parents), although, once again, optimism usually outweighs pessimism. Two of the longest trends we have about children's opportunities, the Roper Starch Worldwide question mentioned above and a Gallup one, present different pictures. The Gallup question, asked in 1946 and in 1997, asks mothers and fathers separately about their daughters' and sons' opportunties to succeed (table 4–3). Sixty-one percent of mothers in 1946 expressed the belief that their daughter's opportunities to succeed would be better than their own. In 1997, even more of mothers surveyed—85 percent—were optimistic, believing that their daughter's opportunities would be better than their own. Slightly more than 60 percent of fathers were optimistic about their son's abilities to do better in both years. In 1946, we as a society were not as far along as we are now in making equal opportunity for women a reality. Given the progress we have made, it is not surprising that mothers are more optimistic about daughters' prospects (table 4–3). But the Roper Starch Worldwide question shows diminishing parental optimism over the past fifty years: only 49 percent believed that their children's opportunities would be better than their own, down from 61 percent in 1939 (table 4–3). Still, optimism outweighed pessimism in 1993, 49 to 32 percent.

Surveys generally reveal more optimism about "your own" children than they do about "most" children. A question shown in table 4–8 asks whether today's youth will have a better life than their parents. In each asking, majorities or near majorities say that it is likely that today's youth will, although more than 40 percent usually said this was somewhat or very unlikely. A Harris question on the same table that asks about "your children" shows a majority in 1996 saying their own children would have a better life, with a quarter saying it would be about as good and 16 percent saying it would be worse. But table 4–9 shows that most people generally expect life for the amorphous "future generation of Americans" to be worse rather than better, although the numbers bounce around. Most people fall in the middle category "only fairly confident," when asked about life for their children compared with their own (table 4–10).

Table 4–11 shows the familiar pattern of greater optimism about *one's own children* than *most children* at two points in time, the late 1930s and the mid-1990s. Tables 4–12 and 4–13 are additional examples of this pattern. We place more weight on people's responses about things they know well such as their children, their neighborhoods, and their schools than we do on their responses about things that are more remote from them (most children, the nation, schools nationally). Table 4–14 summarizes this section well. This survey, taken by the Roper Center at the University of Connecticut for *Reader's Digest* in 1996, poses a long series of questions about how people are getting along and about their expectations for the future. It shows that solid majorities believe their financial status and their standard of living are better than those of their parents. It also shows that majorities expect that when their children are as old as they are, the children will have a higher standard of living. But optimism turns to pessimism when the Roper Center asks about the next generation. A bare majority, 52 percent, say the next generation will be worse off financially than the current generation. Only 29 percent expect it to be better off.

Survey questions about the American Dream are fairly recent. Despite the claims of some, there seems to be very little evidence from the thin collection of surveys on this sense of promise that the dream is eroding. Roper Starch Worldwide found a ten-percentage-point shift in nine years in the belief that the dream was "very much" alive (32 percent in 1986, 22 percent in 1995) and, separately, that it was "not really alive" (11 percent in 1986, 21 percent in 1995) (table 4–15). Majority opinion, however, clustered around the response "somewhat alive," 55 percent in 1986 and 52 percent in 1995. To a question asked by Luntz Research Companies in 1994 and 1996, more than 80 percent said the dream is alive today, with only about one in ten saying it was dead.

Question wording powerfully affects views about whether it is still possible for most people in the country to achieve the dream. A question asked in May 1996 by ABC News and another by Opinion Dynamics for Fox News in February 1997 found substantial majorities that believed the dream could be achieved. A Yankelovich Partners question asking people to affirm a negative—that the American Dream has become almost impossible for most people to achieve—produced majority (negative) support, too (table 4–16). A Roper Starch Worldwide trend shows that people think the dream is harder to attain than a generation ago and will be harder still a generation from now (table 4–17).

Responses to questions that ask whether people have reached or expect to reach the American Dream also shift around, depending on wording and emphasis, but most questions show that most people expect to attain it. Significant numbers say they already have (table 4–18). The Roper Starch Worldwide question in table 4–19 shows how people react to some possible descriptions or definitions of the dream. Owning a home, being able to get a high school education, and being able to live in an open society where everyone has an equal chance were the top-rated descriptions of the dream in 1995. Other surveys that we have not included here show that things such as finding true love (Wirthlin Worldwide), being in a happy relationship (Roper Starch Worldwide), and believing in God (Luntz Research Companies) are thought by many to be part of the American Dream.

TABLE 4–1
HARD WORK AND OPPORTUNITY, 1952–1997
(percent)

QUESTION: Some people say there's not much opportunity in America today—that the average man doesn't have much chance to really get ahead. Others say there's plenty of opportunity, and anyone who works hard can go as far as he wants. How do you feel about this?

	Yes, There's Opportunity	*No, There's Little Opportunity*
1952	87	9

QUESTION: How good a chance do you think a person has to get ahead today, if the person works hard?

	Very Good/ Good Chance	*Some/Little Chance*	*No Chance at All*
1980	63	35	2

QUESTION: America is the land of opportunity where everyone who works hard can get ahead?

	Strongly Agree/ Agree	*Disagree/ Strongly Disagree*
1980	70	31

QUESTION: A basic American belief has been that if you work hard you can get ahead—reach the goals you set and more. Does that still hold true?

	Yes, Still True	*Not True*
1994	74	24

QUESTION: Please tell me whether you strongly agree, somewhat agree, somewhat disagree, or strongly disagree with the following statement . . . In America, if you work hard, you can be anything you want to be.

	Strongly/ Somewhat Agree	*Somewhat/ Strongly Disagree*
1994	74	25

(Table continues)

TABLE 4–1 (continued)

QUESTION: Please tell me whether you strongly agree, somewhat agree, somewhat disagree or strongly disagree with the following statement . . . In America, if you work hard, you can be anything you want to be.

	Strongly/ Somewhat Agree	*Somewhat/ Strongly Disagree*
1996	79	20

QUESTION: People who work hard in this nation are likely to succeed.

	True	*False*
1997	79	18

SOURCES: For first panel, survey by the University of Michigan National Election Survey, 1952. For second and third panels, survey by Kluegel and Smith, *Beliefs about Inequality: Americans' Views of What Is and What Ought to Be* (1980 survey for 1986 book). For fourth panel, survey by the Roper Center for Public Opinion Research/University of Connecticut for *Reader's Digest*, 1994. For fifth and sixth panels, surveys by Luntz Research Companies, 1994, 1996. For seventh panel, survey by Opinion Research Corporation International for *USA Weekend*, 1997.

TABLE 4–2
OPPORTUNITIES FOR AMERICANS COMPARED WITH THE PAST, 1983–1997
(percent)

QUESTION: Since the time this country was settled, the United States has been called the land of opportunity. Do you think there are more opportunities for Americans today than in the past, or fewer opportunities today, or about the same today as in the past?

	More Opportunities	*Fewer Opportunities*	*About the Same*
Jan. 1983	40	34	25
Jan. 1985	52	20	25
June 1986	54	21	22
Oct. 1986	49	24	26
Jan. 1990	47	20	28
Mar. 1996	41	27	30
Sept. 1997	42	22	32

NOTE: Question wording varied slightly.
SOURCES: Surveys by Roper Starch Worldwide (1983–1990, 1997) and CBS News (1996).

TABLE 4–3
OPPORTUNITIES TO SUCCEED, 1939–1997
(percent)

QUESTION: Do you think your opportunities to succeed are better than, or not as good as, those your parents had?
QUESTION: Do you think your [son's/children's] opportunities to succeed will be better than, or not as good as, those you have? (If no children:) Assume that you *did* have children.

	Better	*Not as Good*	*Same*[a]
	Your opportunities compared with your parents		
Dec. 1939[b]	61	20	12
Feb. 1940[b]	59	22	13
Jan. 1947[b, c]	70	13	13
Dec. 1990	70	15	12
Aug. 1993	63	22	11
	Your [son's/children's] opportunities compared with yours		
Dec. 1939[b]	61	15	10
Feb. 1940[b]	60	15	10
Jan. 1947[b, c]	62	13	12
Dec. 1990	61	21	12
Aug. 1993	49	32	10

QUESTION: [Asked of mothers] Will your daughter's opportunities to succeed be better than or not as good as those you've had?
QUESTION: [Asked of fathers] Will your son's opportunities to succeed be better than or not as good as those you've had?

	Better	*Not as Good*	*Same*[a]
	Mother's opinions of daughter's opportunities		
1946	61	20	12
1997	85	7	6

(Table continues)

TABLE 4–3 (continued)

	Better	*Not as Good*	*Same*[a]
	Father's opinions of son's opportunities		
1946	64	13	13
1997	62	21	11

a. Volunteered response.
b. Question asked only about father's/son's opportunities to succeed. Married people without sons were asked to assume they had a son. Single women were not asked this question.
c. Sample is men only.
SOURCES: For first panel, surveys by Roper Starch Worldwide, latest that of August 1993. For second panel, surveys by the Gallup Organization, latest that of February 1997.

TABLE 4–4

BETTER PREPARED TO GET AHEAD THAN PARENTS, 1939 AND 1990 (percent)

QUESTION: Do you think you are better or less prepared to get ahead than your parents were?

	Better	*Less*	*Same*[a]
1939	72	9	13
1990	76	10	10

a. Volunteered response.
SOURCES: Surveys by Elmo Roper for *Fortune* (1939) and Roper Starch Worldwide (1990).

TABLE 4–5
COMPARING GENERATIONS' FINANCIAL SITUATION, 1980–1996
(percent)

QUESTION: Think of your parents when they were your age. Would you say you are better off financially than they were or not?
QUESTION: And what about your children? Do you think they will be better off than you are financially when they reach your age, or not? [For people who say they have no children, ask: Suppose you did have children, do you think those children would be better off financially or not when they reach your age?]

	Better Off	*Not Better Off*
	In comparison with your parents at your age	
Apr. 1980	88	10
Mar. 1981	64	35
Dec. 1981	69	28
Mar. 1982	69	30
Jan. 1983	70	29
Nov. 1983	77	21
Dec. 1983	73	25
Jan. 1985	74	23
Mar. 1985	75	23
Mar. 1986	81	18
Apr. 1986	78	21
May 1986	82	17
May 1991	70	26
Jan. 1995	67	31
Jan. 1996	67	30
Mar. 1996	70	29
May 1996	69	29
	When they reach your age, your children will be	
Mar. 1981	47	43
Mar. 1982	43	41
Jan. 1983	44	45
Nov. 1983	62	27
Dec. 1983	65	29
Jan. 1985	62	29

(Table continues)

TABLE 4–5 (continued)

	Better Off	*Not Better Off*
Mar. 1986	74	19
Apr. 1986	69	26
May 1986	71	23
May 1991	66	25
Jan. 1995	54	39
Jan. 1996	52	39
Mar. 1996	52	42
May 1996	60	33

SOURCE: Surveys by ABC News/*Washington Post,* latest that of May 1996.

TABLE 4–6
COMPARING GENERATIONS' STANDARD OF LIVING, 1989–1995
(percent)

QUESTION: Do you think your standard of living is higher, lower, or about the same as your parents' standard of living?
QUESTION: Now, looking into the future, do you think your children's standard of living will be higher, lower, or about the same as your standard of living?

	Higher	*Lower*	*About the Same*
	Your standard of living is		
1989	59	19	20
1992	59	19	21
1993	57	18	23
1994	55	20	24
1995	58	20	21
	Your children's standard of living will be		
1989	52	12	19
1992	47	15	28
1993	49	17	27
1994	43	22	28
1995	46	17	29

NOTE: Category "don't have children" not shown above.
SOURCE: Surveys by Cambridge Reports/Research International, latest that of January 1995.

TABLE 4–7
COMPARING GENERATIONS' QUALITY OF LIFE, 1994 AND 1996
(percent)

QUESTION: How does your generation's quality of life compare with your [parents' generation/children's generation]? Is it much better, somewhat better, somewhat worse, much worse or about the same?
QUESTION: How does your generation's standard of living compare with your [parents' generation/children's generation]? Is it much better, somewhat better, somewhat worse, much worse or about the same?

	Better	*Worse*	*Same*
Your generation compared with your parents' generation			
1994			
Quality of life	64	22	13
Standard of living	68	19	13
1996[a]			
Quality of life	74	21	3
Standard of living	74	22	3
Your generation compared with your children's generation			
1994			
Quality of life	44	16	31
Standard of living	49	20	26
1996[a, b]			
Quality of life	48	44	4
Standard of living	48	45	4

NOTE: Categories combined.
a. Question wording does not include the "about the same" option.
b. Compares *next generation's* quality of life and standard of living with your own rather than *your children's* quality of life and standard of living.
SOURCE: Surveys by Luntz Research Companies, latest that of November 1996.

TABLE 4–8
LIKELIHOOD FOR TODAY'S YOUTH OF BETTER LIFE THAN PARENTS, 1983–1996
(percent)

QUESTION: In America, each generation has tried to have a better life than their parents, with a better living standard, better homes, a better education, etc. How likely do you think it is that today's youth will have a better life than their parents—very likely, somewhat likely, somewhat unlikely, or very unlikely?

	Poll	*Very Likely*	*Somewhat Likely*	*Somewhat Unlikely*	*Very Unlikely*
Jan. 1983	RSW	19	35	27	17
Jan. 1985	RSW	28	40	19	10
Jan. 1990	RSW	21	41	20	13
Oct. 1992	RSW	28	46	13	4
Dec. 1995	*NYT*	11	38	32	17
Sept. 1996	CBS/*NYT*	16	42	27	13
Oct. 1996	CBS/*NYT*	11	40	32	14
Nov. 1996	CBS/*NYT*	15	41	27	15
Dec. 1996	*NYT*	14	37	30	17
Jan. 1998	CBS/*NYT*	18	47	26	8

QUESTION: Do you expect that your children will have a better life than you have had, a worse life, or a life about as good as yours?

	Better	*Worse*	*About as Good*
1989	59	10	25
1992	31	28	37
1996	50	16	26

SOURCES: For first panel, surveys by Roper Starch Worldwide and CBS News/*New York Times*. For second panel, surveys by Louis Harris and Associates, latest that of February 1996.

TABLE 4–9
EXPECTATIONS FOR FUTURE GENERATIONS, 1989–1998
(percent)

QUESTION: Do you think the future generation of Americans will be better off, worse off, or about the same as people today?

	Poll	*Better*	*Worse*	*Same*
June 1989	CBS/*NYT*	25	52	18
June 1990	CBS/*NYT*	28	36	31
Mar. 1991	CBS/*NYT*	36	26	35
Oct. 1991	CBS/*NYT*	20	52	25
Nov. 1991	CBS/*NYT*	26	43	28
Sept. 1992	CBS/*NYT*	22	46	21
Oct. 1992	CBS/*NYT*	26	44	20
Nov. 1992[a]	VRS	30	35	30
Dec. 1992	CBS/*NYT*	25	40	31
Feb. 1993	CBS/*NYT*	22	49	22
Aug. 1994	Luntz	32	46	18
Nov. 1994	CBS/*NYT*	18	57	21
Dec. 1994	CBS/*NYT*	21	47	30
Mar. 1995	CBS/*NYT*	16	58	20
Aug. 1996	CBS/*NYT*	16	48	31
Sept. 1996	CBS/*NYT*	24	38	32
Oct. 1996	ABC	31	34	33
Nov. 1996[a]	VNS	30	34	36
Feb. 1997	CBS	14	51	31
Jan. 1998	CBS/*NYT*	28	38	31
Mar. 1998	CBS	29	41	23

NOTE: Question wording varies slightly.
a. Sample is national adult voters leaving the polls.
SOURCES: Surveys by CBS News/*New York Times*, Voter Research and Surveys (ABC News, Cable News Network, CBS News, NBC News), Luntz Research Companies, ABC News, and the Voter News Service (ABC News, Associated Press, Cable News Network, CBS News, Fox News, NBC News).

TABLE 4–10
CONFIDENCE ABOUT LIFE FOR YOUR CHILDREN, 1973–1995
(percent)

QUESTION: Now, taking some specific aspects of our life, we'd like to know how confident you feel about them. Do you feel very confident, only fairly confident, or not at all confident that life for your children will be better than it has been for us?

	Very Confident	*Only Fairly Confident*	*Not at All Confident*
1973	26	36	30
1974	25	41	28
1975	23	39	32
1976	31	39	25
1979	25	41	29
1982	20	44	32
1983	24	38	33
1988	20	45	28
1992	17	46	31
1995	17	44	34

SOURCE: Surveys by Roper Starch Worldwide, latest that of September 1995.

TABLE 4–11
FUTURE FOR YOUR CHILDREN COMPARED WITH THAT FOR MOST CHILDREN, 1937–1996
(percent)

QUESTION: Do you think the opportunities for getting ahead today are greater, or not so great, as they were in your father's day?

	Greater	*Not So Great*	*Same*[a]
1937	47	38	15

QUESTION: Do you think the opportunities for most young men to get ahead today are as good as they were thirty years ago?

	Yes	*No*
1939	34	60

QUESTION: Looking to the future, when your children grow up do you think they will be better off or worse off than you are now?
QUESTION: Looking to the future, do you think *most* children in this country will grow up to be better off or worse off than their parents?

	Better	*Worse*	*Same*[a]
Your children[b]			
1994	47	39	5
1996	51	41	4
Most children			
1994[c]	33	50	6
1996	38	55	3

a. Volunteered response.
b. Based on sample of parents with children under eighteen.
c. Based on sample of nonparents only.
SOURCES: For first panel, survey by the Gallup Organization, August 1937. For second panel, survey by the Gallup Organization, February 1939. For third panel, surveys by Princeton Survey Research Associates for *Newsweek* (1994) and the Pew Research Center for the People & the Press (1996).

TABLE 4–12
YOUR CHILDREN'S GENERATION'S STANDARD OF LIVING, 1990–1998
(percent)

QUESTION: Do you expect your children's generation to enjoy a higher standard of living than your generation?

	Yes	*No*
May 1990[a]	60	37
July 1994	45	50
Sept. 1994	49	45
Dec. 1994	48	46
Mar. 1995	49	45
Jan. 1996	41	52
Mar. 1996	41	51
June 1996[a]	43	47
Sept. 1996[a]	43	47
Apr. 1997	52	44
June 1997	53	42
Feb. 1998	64	32

a. Registered voters.
SOURCES: Surveys by NBC News/*Wall Street Journal* (1990–1994, 1996–1998) and Hart/Teeter Research for the Council for Excellence in Government (1995).

TABLE 4–13
STANDARD OF LIVING FOR NEXT GENERATION, 1991–1996
(percent)

QUESTION: Do you expect the next generation of Americans will have a better standard of living than the one we have now, a worse standard of living than now, or about the same standard of living as we have now?

	Better	*Worse*	*Same*
Nov. 1991	20	51	23
Oct. 1992	24	36	36
Jan. 1993	23	38	35
June 1993	14	51	32
Dec. 1993	15	47	35
Oct. 1995	13	51	33
Aug. 1996	18	46	33

SOURCE: Surveys by the *Los Angeles Times*, latest that of August 1996.

TABLE 4–14
EXPECTATIONS AND ACCOMPLISHMENTS, 1996
(percent)

QUESTION: Do you agree or disagree with the following: In America today, people like me [and my family or spouse] have a good chance of improving our standard of living?

Agree	*Disagree*
70	27

QUESTION: Considering your entire adult life, do you think you've gotten ahead financially, fallen behind financially, or stayed about the same?

Gotten Ahead	*Fallen Behind*	*Stayed Same*
54	18	29

QUESTION: Is your financial standard of living—which includes your house and lifestyle as well as your income—higher than your parents achieved during their peak financial years, lower, or about the same?

Higher	*Lower*	*About the Same*
56	22	21

QUESTION: Considering income, as well as homes and lifestyles, do you think that your generation is enjoying a higher economic standard of living than your parents' generation, a lower economic standard of living, or about the same as your parents' generation?

Higher	*Lower*	*About the Same*
64	16	19

QUESTION: All in all, are you [and your spouse] better off financially than your parents were when they were your age, about the same, or worse off financially than your parents were when they were your age?

Better	*Worse*	*About the Same*
59	17	21

(Table continues)

TABLE 4–14 (continued)

QUESTION: Some people say although there are many economic hardships faced by every generation in America, eventually most will do better financially than their parents. Thinking about your own generation, do you think it is true that eventually most people in your generation will do better financially than their parents, or not?

Will Do Better	*Most Will Not Do Better*
70	23

QUESTION: Do you feel that you, personally, will eventually do better financially than your parents, or not?

Yes	*No*
70	19

QUESTION: Do you think that by the time they are your age, your children will have a higher financial standard of living than you have now, a lower one, or about the same standard of living?

Higher	*Lower*	*About the Same*
53	12	29

QUESTION: Do you think the average American family is better off now economically than the average American family 40 years ago, meaning the 1950s, or not?

Better Off Now	*Better Off in the 1950s*
59	31

QUESTION: How about compared to 20 years ago, meaning the 1970s?

Better Off Now	*Better Off in the 1970s*
46	38

QUESTION: Do you think that the next generation will be better off financially or worse off financially than the current generation?

Better	*Worse Off*	*About the Same*[a]
29	52	8

NOTE: Sample is adults thirty years old and over.

a. Volunteered response.

SOURCE: Survey by the Roper Center for Public Opinion Research/University of Connecticut for *Reader's Digest*, 1996.

TABLE 4–15
THE AMERICAN DREAM, ALIVE OR DEAD? 1986–1996
(percent)

QUESTION: I'd like to talk with you now about a term with which you are probably familiar—*the American Dream.* Do you personally feel that the American Dream is very much alive today, somewhat alive, or not really alive?

	Very Much Alive	*Somewhat Alive*	*Not Really Alive*
1986	32	55	11
1990	23	50	20
1992	16	52	26
1993	20	50	22
1995	22	52	21

QUESTION: Do you think that the American Dream is very much alive today, somewhat alive today or is it dead?

	Very Much Alive	*Somewhat Alive*	*Dead*
1994	23	64	12
1996	20	66	11

QUESTION: I'd like to talk to you now about a term with which you probably are familiar—*the American Dream.* Do you believe in the American Dream, or not?

	Yes, Believe	*No, Don't Believe*
1995		
White	79	17
African Americans	67	30
Asians	75	22
Latinos	68	21
National	76	19

SOURCES: For first panel, surveys by Roper Starch Worldwide, latest that of December 1995. For second panel, surveys by Luntz Research Companies, latest that of November 1996. For third panel, survey by Kaiser Family Foundation/Harvard University/*Washington Post,* September 1995.

TABLE 4–16

IS THE AMERICAN DREAM STILL POSSIBLE? 1995–1998

(percent)

QUESTION: Do you think it's still possible for most people in this country to achieve the American Dream, or do you think that's not possible anymore?

	Still Possible	*Not Possible*
1996	71	26

QUESTION: Do you think that if an individual works hard, they can still achieve the American Dream of making a decent living, owning a home, and sending their children to college?

	Yes	*No*
1997	72	24

QUESTION: Do you agree or disagree . . . The American Dream has become impossible for most people to achieve.

	Agree	*Disagree*
1995	57	40
1996	63	34
1997	55	41
1998	51	45

QUESTION: In today's society, do you think the American Dream is achievable for all Americans who are willing to work for it; for most Americans, but not all; only for some Americans; or for very few Americans, even if they are willing to work for it?

	All	*Most*	*Only Some*	*Very Few*
1995	33	29	22	15
1997	30	29	24	16

SOURCES: For first panel, survey by ABC News, May 1996. For second panel, survey by Opinion Dynamics/Fox News, February 1997. For third panel, surveys by Yankelovich Partners, latest that of January 1998. For fourth panel, surveys by Hart/Teeter Research for the Council for Excellence in Government, latest that of February 1997.

TABLE 4–17
THE AMERICAN DREAM COMPARED WITH THE PAST AND LOOKING TO THE FUTURE, 1986–1998
(percent)

QUESTION: Compared with the past—say, a generation ago—do you feel the American Dream is easier to attain today, harder to attain, or is it about the same?
QUESTION: Looking to the future—say, a generation from now—do you feel the American Dream will be easier to attain than today, harder to attain, or will it be about the same?

	Poll	Easier to Attain	Harder to Attain	About the Same
		Compared with the past		
Oct. 1986[a]	RSW	23	45	32
Dec. 1990	RSW	17	61	18
May 1992	RSW	8	72	18
Dec. 1993	RSW	13	64	19
Dec. 1995	RSW	12	63	22
		Looking to the future		
Oct. 1986[a]	RSW	10	55	33
Dec. 1990	RSW	13	62	19
July 1993	PSRA	6	67	24
Dec. 1993	RSW	8	64	21
Aug. 1994[b]	Luntz	14	78	4
Dec. 1995	RSW	8	66	20
Aug. 1996[c]	CBS/*NYT*	4	68	24
Nov. 1996[b]	Luntz	16	77	4
Jan. 1998[c]	CBS/*NYT*	9	55	34

a. In 1986, questions were asked of the 87 percent of respondents who believed the American Dream still had meaning. A special analysis found that the difference in the bases had a negligible impact on the results, which are now based on the total.
b. Question wording varied and did not include the option of "about the same." Four percent volunteered it nonetheless.
c. Question wording varied slightly.
SOURCES: Surveys by Roper Starch Worldwide, Princeton Survey Research Associates for *Family Circle*, Luntz Research Companies, and CBS News/*New York Times*.

TABLE 4–18

WHERE YOU ARE ON THE ROAD TO THE AMERICAN DREAM, 1992–1997 (percent)

QUESTION: Do you think you will reach, as you define it, the American Dream in your lifetime, or have you already reached it?
QUESTION: Did your parents reach the American Dream? Your children or the next generation—do you feel they will reach the American Dream?

	1992	*1995*
Have already reached the American Dream	37	45
Will reach it in my lifetime	43	35
Will not reach it in my lifetime	17	16
Parents reached the American Dream	54	55
Did not	43	39
Your children or the next generation will reach the dream	62	59
Will not	29	26

QUESTION: And how close are you to achieving your own [vision/version] of the American Dream? Have you achieved it already, are you close to achieving it, are you very far away, or do you never expect to achieve your [vision/version] of the American Dream?

	Achieved It	*Close*	*Very Far Away*	*Never Expect*
1994	22	49	19	6
1996	20	46	21	9

QUESTION: Do you feel that you have lived the American Dream or have been unable to live the American Dream?

	Have	*Have Not*
1997	65	28

SOURCES: For first panel, surveys by Wirthlin Worldwide, latest that of December 1995. For second panel, surveys by Luntz Research Companies, latest that of November 1996. For third panel, survey by Hart/Teeter Research for the Council for Excellence in Government, February 1997.

TABLE 4–19
DEFINITIONS OF THE AMERICAN DREAM, 1995
(percent)

QUESTION: I'm going to read you some possible definitions or descriptions of the American Dream, and for each one I'd like you to tell me if that's very much what you understand the American Dream to mean, or sort of what it means, or not what it means.

	Very Much	*Sort Of*	*Not*
To own a home	77	18	3
To be able to get a high school education	76	17	5
To live in an open society in which everyone has an equal chance	75	20	4
To have freedom of choice in how to live one's life	71	23	3
To be able to have a financially secure retirement	69	23	6
To be able to have both a rewarding career and family life	67	26	6
To be able to send one's children to college	66	27	5
To be able to get a college education	65	27	6
To be financially secure enough to have ample time for leisure pursuits	63	30	6
To have a job you enjoy	63	30	6
To do better than one's parent did	53	35	9
To be able to rise from clerk or worker to president of a company	52	34	11
To be able to start a business of one's own	51	34	13
To live in a natural environment free from pollution	48	37	13
To be able to become wealthy	43	40	14
To be able to buy all the things one wants	37	39	22

SOURCE: Survey by Roper Starch Worldwide, December 1995.

CHAPTER 5

Politics and Government

Politics and Politicians

Almost as long as the pollsters have been asking questions, Americans have expressed skepticism about politics and politicians. In 1943, in a poll conducted by the National Opinion Research Center at the University of Chicago, 48 percent of those surveyed agreed with the statement, "It is almost impossible for a man to stay honest if he goes into politics," and 42 percent disagreed. When Opinion Dynamics, in a survey for Fox News, asked a similar question in 1997, 55 percent agreed that people who go into politics cannot remain honest, and 37 percent disagreed (table 5–1). In 1936, Gallup reported that nearly two-thirds of those surveyed said that "politics" played a part in relief efforts in their locality.

Since 1945 when Gallup first asked the question, large majorities have said they would not want a son to go into politics as a life's work. In more recent questions, similar strong majorities have felt that way about daughters, too (table 5–2). When Gallup once asked a follow-up question about why people did not want a son to go into politics, "corruption" was the response most frequently given. Polls taken more recently show that people are not enthusiastic about a child's becoming president, either. Interestingly, though, most people believe that their child *could* grow up to be president; it is simply not something they would choose for him or her (table 5–2).

The association of corruption and politics is apparent in responses to other early poll questions. In 1958, when the University of Michigan began asking a jumbled question about the number of corrupt people running government, only about a quarter gave the positive response that "hardly any of the people running the government" were "a little crooked" (table 5–3). In 1997 when Gallup asked the question, only 8 percent gave that response, and 3 percent volunteered that all the people running the government were crooked.

Two recent reports confirm the connection between politics and corruption and people's views about government. An analysis done by Lake Sosin Snell Perry & Associates, Inc., for the Pew Charitable Trusts in November 1995 reported that corruption and dishonesty were the primary reason that people distrusted government.[1] The researchers pointed out that the public does not distinguish between politicians who hold office and bureaucrats. In a Hart/Teeter Research poll for the Council for Excellence in Government in 1997, people were asked to describe in their own words the biggest problems with government today. Thirteen percent volunteered that government was too big; 13 percent also mentioned crooked politicians and corruption.

These reports and others emphasize the public's belief that politicians quickly lose touch with ordinary citizens. Many contemporary polls confirm this insight. Majorities or near majorities of Americans believe their elected officials are not interested in the problems of ordinary Americans and that public officials do not care what ordinary people think (table 5–4).

Government

The next section displays trends in attitudes about the federal government. The United States does not have a strong pro-state tradition. We have tended to put more emphasis than Europeans, for example, on individuals' responsibility to take care of themselves. A question in a poll conducted in 1997 by Hart/Teeter Research for the Council for Excellence in Government illustrates Americans' strong preference for this approach. People were asked which of two statements about the role of government came closer to their own point of view. Two-thirds chose "people are responsible for their own well-being and have an obligation to take care of themselves," and just 16 percent chose "government is responsible for the well-being of all its citizens and it has an obligation to help people" (table 5–5). When the *Los Angeles Times* asked that question a

1. *The Show Me Nation: Restoring Trust in Government* (Survey by Lake Sosin Snell Perry & Associates, Inc., for the Pew Charitable Trusts), Washington, D.C., 1995.

decade earlier, the results were similar. Sixty-seven percent put the emphasis on the individual; 24 percent, on government.

To say that people are basically responsible for themselves is not to say that people are fundamentally antigovernment. Different eras require different levels of government activity, as polling data clearly show. In a 1939 survey for *Fortune,* Elmo Roper asked people about different areas where government might have a role. In the essay accompanying the survey, Roper "guesses" about what such a survey would have shown a decade earlier, when polls did not exist. "It is safe to say that in 1929 a minimum of government in business was the popular rule," he wrote. "Today, in spite of the trend toward enlargement of government this reliance on laissez faire still seems to prevail among the majority of the people. In 1929 beneficence would probably not have been accepted as a proper function for the federal government. But today it is emphatically held desirable." Roper's insight about changing preferences based on objective conditions is an important one.

The view of government's proper role in the society expanded during the Great Depression and into the New Deal. Although a favorable disposition toward federal government activity prevailed in the early days of the Great Society, there were signs even then that skepticism toward more government was growing. Today, people emphatically reject the idea of more government as the answer to the nation's problems. But they are not ready to shut the federal government down. The microinitiatives first offered by President Clinton in the 1996 campaign have been broadly popular. Still, efforts to expand government substantially will be greeted with much more skepticism than in the past. Several new polls show that people reject the idea of a government of bare essentials, described in one poll as providing for the country's defense and for the fair administration of justice. But they do not want a full-service government either (table 5–6).

Most Americans are skeptical of President Clinton's claim, made in his 1996 State of the Union speech, that "the era of big government is over." In January 1998, Opinion Dynamics, in a survey for Fox News, reminded people of the president's words and then asked them whether it was really over. Just 6 percent thought it was, but 85 percent disagreed.

In the past few years, largely in response to the Oklahoma City bombing and the attention given to the militia movement, a number of pollsters have tried to explore animosity toward government. Fewer than 10 percent see the government as an enemy (table 5–7). Substantial numbers of people, however, see a certain utility in distrust of government as a check on government's power (table 5–8). People believe that government can have a positive impact on people's lives and that government often does a better job than people give it credit for (table 5–9).

How many significant successes has the federal government had in the past thirty years (see table 5–10)? Only a handful (8 percent) say there have been a large number, but a near majority says there have been a fair number (48 percent). When asked to name the two or three most important successes, people volunteer the military, the space program, welfare, foreign policy, and educational programs—all at low levels of positive awareness. In evaluating specific goals the federal government has pursued, people give the government decent marks in quite a few areas. Large majorities say the government has been very or fairly successful in promoting space exploration, providing for the national defense, keeping the nation at peace, maintaining a growing economy, protecting the environment, supporting medical research, making health care available to senior citizens, regulating business to protect consumers and employees, protecting the rights of individuals, and preventing discrimination based on race or sex. A near majority says the federal government has been successful at supporting quality public education. But solid majorities say the government has been fairly or very unsuccessful in reducing poverty, reducing crime, improving moral values, controlling illegal immigration, and reducing drug abuse.

People are not viscerally opposed to government, then, but their evaluation of it today contains substantial criticism. Although Americans believe government can have a positive effect, they do not believe it is having a positive effect now. In a January 1998 CBS News/*New York Times* poll, just 31 percent said it is (table 5–11). Forty percent said government was having a negative impact, and around two in ten said that it was not having much impact. Large numbers report that they are dissatisfied with the way the federal government is performing today (table 5–12), a view that probably contributes to the spike since 1973 in the number of people (now around 60 percent) who believe the best government is one that governs least (table 5–13).

People believe that the power and reach of the federal government have grown significantly. In 1936, 56 percent told Gallup interviewers that they favored the theory of government that concentrated more power in the hands of the federal government, and 44 percent the one that placed more power in the hands of state government. In 1941, about a third told Gallup interviewers that the federal government in Washington had too much power, but a majority, 56 percent, disagreed (table 5–14). As late as 1964, more people told University of Michigan interviewers that the government in Washington was not getting too strong (36 percent) than said the government was getting too powerful for the good of the country and the individual (30 percent), but by 1966, a plurality said the government in Washington was becoming too powerful. In 1992, only 17 percent said that the government was not getting too strong. Opinion Dynamics, in a poll in July 1997 for Fox News, asked a question similar to the one Gallup asked in 1941; 64 percent said that the government in Washington has too much power.

Americans distrust concentrations of power generally, but the number saying that big government and not big business or big labor presents the greatest threat to the country today has soared since 1959 when the question was first asked (table 5–15). The Pew Research Center asks about whether the federal government controls too much of our daily lives, and today around three in ten are in complete agreement (table 5–16).

Another strike against government these days is that people are not very confident in the federal government's ability to solve problems. The last time this question was asked in 1996, only 6 percent had a great deal of confidence, 35 percent had a fair amount, 42 percent voiced not very much, and 15 percent had no confidence at all (table 5–17). More devastating perhaps is the strong majoritarian view that the federal government actually creates more problems than it solves (table 5–18).

In their analysis of distrust of government, Fred Steeper and Christoper Blunt identified the belief that government wastes too much of our money as particularly devastating.[2] In their Market Strategies survey, 93 percent held that view, eight in ten of them strongly. According to Steeper and Blunt, "It is difficult to conceive of an attitude shared as universally as this one, or a more clearly articulated explanation for the public's frustration with our leaders in Washington." In many other surveys conducted over a long

2. *The Discontent and Cynicism of the American Public: Analysis of Trust in Government Attitudes* (Report by Fred Steeper and Christopher Blunt, Market Strategies), Southfield, Michigan, August 1995.

period, people say that government wastes a lot of our tax money. Around six in ten now see government as almost always wasteful and inefficient (table 5–19). When survey organizations have asked how much of every dollar collected by Washington is wasted, the median response over the past decade has been around fifty cents.

Not surprisingly, given the broad and deep criticism of government performance, people's trust in government to do the right thing is low (table 5–20). There is a strong belief that government is run by a few big interests, not for the benefit of all (table 5–21). People believe that the federal government is doing too many things, and, at least in the abstract, they say they prefer a smaller government with fewer services to a larger one with many services (tables 5–22, 5–23, and 5–24).

Americans' views about politicians and their skepticism of government help to explain the support we see in so many surveys for such constraints on the power of government as term limits. Part of this view reflects a deeply ingrained suspicion of federal government power, but part of it is a response to increasingly negative views of federal government performance.

Democracies need vigorous criticism, and, as we have seen in this chapter, the public offers a truckload. But we should not overlook the findings in table 5–25. When the Pew Research Center asked in late 1997 which of three statements came closest to people's views about the federal government, 37 percent said that it needed very major reform, but a solid majority, 58 percent, said that it was basically sound and needed only some reform. In spite of the stinging criticism of federal government performance, great majorities of Americans continue to believe that, for all its faults, the United States has the best system of government in the world. Its current performance is the problem, not the institutional structure.

TABLE 5-1
IS IT POSSIBLE TO STAY HONEST IN POLITICS? 1943 AND 1997 (percent)

QUESTION: It has been said that it is almost impossible for a man to stay honest if he goes into politics. Do you agree or disagree?
QUESTION: Do you believe honest government is impossible?
QUESTION: Would you agree or disagree . . . People who go into politics cannot remain honest?

	Agree/ Yes	*Disagree/ No*
Nov. 1943	48	42
July 1997[a]	52	46
Aug. 1997	55	37

NOTE: In 1952, Opinion Research Corporation asked the question: "Do you think there's dishonesty among just a few people in government, or is it widespread?" Forty-one percent said just a few people were dishonest, and 53 percent responded that dishonesty was widespread.
a. Respondents who answered yes above were asked an additional question—"Who do you think is most responsible for dishonest government?" The responses were the voters (8 percent), politicians (66 percent), or the media (15 percent).
SOURCES: Surveys by the National Opinion Research Center (1943) and Opinion Dynamics/Fox News (1997).

TABLE 5–2
SON OR DAUGHTER IN POLITICS OR AS PRESIDENT? 1943–1996
(percent)

QUESTION: If you had a [son or daughter], would you like to see [him or her] go into politics as a life's work?

	Yes	*No*
Son in politics		
1943[a]	17	69
1945[a]	21	68
1953	20	70
1955[a]	27	60
1962[a]	23	69
1965[a]	36	54
1973	23	64
1991	24	72
1993	22	70
1994	25	71
1995	32	63
Daughter in politics		
1991	26	70
1993	24	69
1994	26	71
1995	26	71

QUESTION: Do you think it's possible your child could grow up to be president?
QUESTION: Please tell me whether you strongly agree, somewhat agree, somewhat disagree or strongly disagree with the following statement . . . Any child born in America can grow up to be president.

	Poll	*Yes/Agree*	*No/Disagree*
1988	AP/MG	59	34
1992	ABC/*WP*	52	48
1996	Luntz	60	39

(Table continues)

TABLE 5–2 (continued)

QUESTION: Would you want your child to grow up to be president?
QUESTION: Now I have some questions about the office of U.S. president . . . Would you want your child to grow up to be president, or not?
QUESTION: Would you like your child or one of your children to grow up and be president?

	Poll	*Yes/Agree*	*No/Disagree*
1988	AP/MG	41	46
1992	ABC/*WP*	35	61
1996	PSRA/KR	32	63
1996	Yank.	37	61

a. Question wording was: " . . . as life's work when he gets out of school?"
SOURCES: For first panel, surveys by the National Opinion Research Center (1943) and the Gallup Organization (1945–1995). For second panel, surveys by Associated Press/Media General, ABC News/*Washington Post,* and Luntz Research Companies. For third panel, surveys by Associated Press/Media General, ABC News/*Washington Post,* Princeton Survey Research Associates for Knight Ridder, and Yankelovich Partners.

TABLE 5–3
ARE CROOKED PEOPLE RUNNING GOVERNMENT? 1958–1997
(percent)

QUESTION: Do you think that quite a few of the people running the government are a little crooked, not very many are, or do you think hardly any of them are crooked at all?

	Poll	*Quite a Few*	*Not Many*	*Hardly Any*	*All Are Crooked*[a]
1958	Mich.	24	44	26	—
1964	Mich.	29	49	18	—
1968	Mich.	25	52	19	—
1970	Mich.	32	49	16	—
1972	Mich.	36	45	14	—
1974	Mich.	45	42	10	—
1976	Mich.	42	40	13	—
1978	Mich.	39	42	13	—
1980	Mich.	47	41	9	—
1981	*LAT*	39	43	15	—
1984	Mich.	32	50	14	—
1988	Mich.	40	45	11	—
1990	Mich.	48	40	9	—
1991	ABC/*WP*	46	42	11	—
1991	NBC/*WSJ*[b]	63	27	7	—
1992	Mich.	46	44	9	—
1992	Gallup	61	25	7	4
1992	NBC/*WSJ*[b]	64	26	8	—
1992	NBC/*WSJ*	62	29	8	—
1994	Mich.	51	39	8	—
1994	Gallup	58	29	6	5
1996	Mich.	43	47	9	—
1996	Gallup	47	33	12	5
1996	Gallup	52	32	9	5
1997	Gallup	50	37	8	3

a. Volunteered response.
b. Registered voters.
SOURCES: Surveys by the University of Michigan National Election Studies, the *Los Angeles Times*, ABC News/*Washington Post*, NBC News/*Wall Street Journal*, and the Gallup Organization.

TABLE 5–4
PUBLIC OFFICIALS DON'T CARE WHAT PEOPLE LIKE ME THINK, 1952–1997
(percent)

QUESTION: Do you agree or disagree with the following statements . . . I don't think public officials care much what people like me think.

	Poll	*Agree*	*Disagree*	*Neither Agree nor Disagree*[a]
1952	Mich.	35	63	—
1956	Mich.	26	71	—
1960	Mich.	25	73	—
1964	Mich.	36	62	—
1966	Mich.	34	57	—
1968	Mich.	43	55	—
1970	Mich.	47	50	—
1972	Mich.	49	49	—
1974	Mich.	50	46	—
1976	Mich.	51	44	—
June 1976	CBS/*NYT*	60	32	—
Sept. 1976	CBS/*NYT*	53	37	—
Oct. 1976	CBS/*NYT*	49	40	—
Oct. 1976	CBS/*NYT*	57	35	—
Apr. 1977	CBS/*NYT*	64	29	—
1978	Mich.	51	45	—
Sept. 1978	CBS	52	42	—
1980	Mich.	52	43	—
Oct. 1980	CBS/*NYT*	51	45	—
1982	Mich.	47	50	—
July 1983	ABC	48	49	—
Dec. 1983	ABC	58	41	—
1984	Mich.	42	57	—
July 1984	Gallup	53	41	—
Feb. 1985	CBS/*NYT*	58	37	—
1986	Mich.	52	43	—
1988	Mich.	51	37	11
1990	Mich.	63	23	13
Sept. 1990	ABC/*WP*	65	34	—
Oct. 1991	ABC/*WP*	58	40	—
1992	Mich.	52	37	10
Apr. 1992	ABC	65	34	—

(Table continues)

TABLE 5–4 (continued)

	Poll	*Agree*	*Disagree*	*Neither Agree nor Disagree*[a]
Sept. 1992	Gallup	59	38	—
Oct. 1992	*WP*	57	41	—
1994	Mich.	66	23	11
Mar. 1994	ABC/*WP*	67	32	—
Dec. 1995	Kaiser	68	31	—
1996	Mich.	60	24	14
Apr. 1996	Gallup	69	31	—
Nov. 1996	Gallup	56	41	—

QUESTION: As I read each pair, tell me whether the first or second statement comes closer to your own views—even if neither is exactly right . . . "Most elected officials care what people like me think" *or* "Most elected officials don't care what people like me think."

	Care What I Think	*Don't Care What I Think*
July 1994	34	64
Oct. 1994	29	68
Apr. 1995	32	64
Oct. 1995	33	64
Oct. 1996	38	58

QUESTION: For each statement, please tell me if you completely agree with it, mostly agree with it, mostly disagree with it or completely disagree with it . . . Most elected officials care what people like me think.

	Completely Agree	*Mostly Agree*	*Mostly Disagree*	*Completely Disagree*
1987	5	42	40	9
1988	5	42	40	11
1989	5	39	42	12
1990	7	37	39	14
1991	7	29	39	23
1992	5	31	46	16
1993	5	35	42	16
1994	4	29	41	25
1997	6	35	38	19

(Table continues)

TABLE 5–4 (continued)

QUESTION: Please tell me if you agree or disagree with the statement . . . People like me don't have any say about what the government does.

	Agree	*Disagree*
July 1983	41	57
Dec. 1983	49	51
Oct. 1991	47	52
Apr. 1992	46	54
Mar. 1994	57	42
May 1996	40	59
Nov. 1997	46	53

QUESTION: For each statement, please tell me if you completely agree with it, mostly agree with it, mostly disagree with it or completely disagree with it . . . Generally speaking, elected officials in Washington lose touch with the people pretty quickly.

	Completely Agree	*Mostly Agree*	*Mostly Disagree*	*Completely Disagree*
1987	22	51	21	3
1988	26	50	19	3
1989	30	50	16	2
1990	30	48	17	2
1991	41	43	11	4
1992	35	49	12	3
1993	29	53	13	3
1994	39	44	13	3

QUESTION: As I read each pair, tell me whether the first or second statement comes closer to your own views—even if neither is exactly right . . . "Elected officials in Washington lose touch with the people pretty quickly" *or* "Elected officials in Washington try hard to stay in touch with the voters back home."

	Officials Lose Touch	*Officials Stay in Touch*
July 1994	71	25
Oct. 1994	74	22
Apr. 1995	76	21
Oct. 1995	73	24
Apr. 1996	72	23
Oct. 1996	69	25

(Table continues)

TABLE 5–4 (continued)

QUESTION: Now I'm going to read you several more statements. Some people agree with a statement, others disagree. As I read each one, tell me whether you more or less agree with it, or more or less disagree . . . Most public officials [people in public office] are not really interested in the problems of the average man.

	Agree	*Disagree*
1973	59	41
1974	66	34
1976	66	34
1977	65	35
1980	72	28
1982	68	32
1984	70	30
1985	64	36
1987	70	30
1988	67	33
1989	66	34
1990	69	31
1991	70	30
1993	75	25
1994	75	25

a. The option "neither agree nor disagree" was introduced in 1988 and has affected distributions. Question wording varied slightly over the years.

SOURCES: For first panel, surveys by the University of Michigan National Election Studies, CBS News/*New York Times*, ABC News/*Washington Post*, the Gallup Organization, and the Kaiser Family Foundation/Harvard University/*Washington Post*. For second and sixth panels, surveys by the Times Mirror/Pew Research Center for the People & the Press, latest that of October 1996. For third and fifth panels, surveys by the Times Mirror/Pew Research Center for the People & the Press. For fourth panel, surveys by ABC News/*Washington Post* (1983–1996) and the Pew Research Center for the People & the Press (1997). For seventh panel, surveys by the National Opinion Research Center, latest that of 1994.

TABLE 5–5
Government versus Personal Responsibility, 1983–1997
(percent)

Question: Which statement comes closer to your view: "The government is responsible for the well-being of all its citizens and it has an obligation to help people when they are in trouble" *or* "People are responsible for their own well-being and they have an obligation to take care of themselves when they are in trouble"?

	Government Is Responsible	*People Are Responsible*
Sept. 1983	43	46
Jan. 1985	39	55
Apr. 1985[a]	24	67
Apr. 1989	42	50
Dec. 1989	45	48
Dec. 1990	43	52
June 1993	45	47
Jan. 1995	43	50
Oct. 1995	42	49
Feb. 1997[a]	16	66

a. Question omitted the words "when they are in trouble."
Sources: Surveys by the *Los Angeles Times* (1983–1995) and Hart/Teeter Research for the Council for Excellence in Government (1997).

TABLE 5–6
THE ROLE OF GOVERNMENT, 1996 AND 1997
(percent)

QUESTION: Thinking about the extent of the role that government plays in the lives of people—which of these best describes your view of how much government should do? "Other than providing for national defense and the fair administration of justice, government should do *as little as possible* to interfere in the lives of people"; "In addition to providing for national defense and the fair administration of justice, the government should work to protect the average American, providing a *safety net* in case something bad happens over which they have little control"; "In addition to everything just mentioned, government should *guarantee* a decent standard of living for everyone, including job creation and . . . basic housing."

	As Little as Possible	*Provide Safety Net*	*Guarantee Standard*
1996	24	34	39

QUESTION: Which of the following is closest to your own thinking about the proper role of the federal government?

	1996	*1997*
Government should solve problems and protect people from adversity.	13	12
Government should help people equip themselves to solve their own problems.	53	52
Government should stay out of people's lives so they can solve their problems without interference or regulation.	30	34

NOTE: In a September 1964 Louis Harris and Associates survey, 68 percent agreed that the "government must see that no one is without food, clothing, or shelter." Thirty-two percent disagreed. The Pew Research Center for the People & the Press updated the question in September-October 1997 and found that 72 percent agreed with the statement while 27 percent disagreed.
SOURCES: For first panel, survey by the Tarrance Group and Lake Research for *U.S. News & World Report*, November 1996. For second panel, surveys by Penn, Schoen & Berland Associates, Inc., for the Democratic Leadership Council, latest that of July 1997.

TABLE 5–7
Government, Friend or Enemy? 1995
(percent)

Question: How do you personally view the federal government in Washington: as an enemy, as a friend, or as neither?

	Friend	*Enemy*	*Neither*	*Both*[a]
1995	29	8	61	1

Question: On another subject, if you had to say, would you say you think of the federal government as your friend or as your enemy, or don't you think about it in those terms?

	Friend	*Enemy*	*Don't Think in Those Terms*
1995	26	6	67

Question: Would you say you're afraid of the federal government, or not afraid of it?

	Not Afraid	*Afraid*
1995	88	12

a. Volunteered response.
Sources: For first panel, survey by the Gallup Organization, August 1995. For second and third panels, survey by ABC News/*Washington Post*, May 1995.

TABLE 5–8
THE UTILITY OF DISTRUST, 1995 AND 1997
(percent)

QUESTION: Do you think that, in the end, it is good or bad that Americans distrust their government as much as they do?

	Good Thing	*Bad Thing*
1995	34	51

QUESTION: Please tell me which one of the following statements about people's attitudes toward the federal government comes closer to your own point of view: "It's a good thing for America that many people are skeptical about the federal government, and we need to guard against government getting too big and powerful" *or* "It's a bad thing for America that many people are skeptical about the federal government, and we need to appreciate what government does and try to improve it."

	Good Thing	*Bad Thing*
1997	53	37

SOURCES: For first panel, survey by Lake Sosin Snell Perry & Associates, Inc., for the Pew Charitable Trusts, October 1995. For second panel, survey by Hart/Teeter Research for the Council for Excellence in Government, February 1997.

TABLE 5-9
CAN GOVERNMENT HAVE A POSITIVE IMPACT? 1995–1998
(percent)

QUESTION: Do you think the government can have a positive impact on people's lives, or not?

	Can Have Positive Impact	*Cannot*
Feb. 1995	89	10
Feb. 1996	87	10
Aug. 1996	89	8
Oct. 1996	88	9
Feb. 1997	88	9
Jan. 1998	87	11

QUESTION: Please tell me if you agree or disagree with the statement . . . A lot of people complain about the government without thinking about the government programs that benefit them.

	Agree	*Disagree*
1996	77	21

QUESTION: Do you completely agree, mostly agree, mostly disagree, or completely disagree that government often does a better job than people give it credit for?

	Completely/ Mostly Agree	*Mostly/Completely Disagree*
1996	60	40

QUESTION: Here are some reasons why people mistrust the government in Washington. For each one, please tell me if you agree, disagree, or are neutral about it . . . People are distrustful of almost all institutions today; there is no special reason to distrust the U.S. government more than other institutions.

	Agree	*Disagree*	*Neutral*
1995	51	32	15

SOURCES: For first panel, surveys by CBS News (1995, Aug. 1996–1997) and CBS News/*New York Times* (Feb. 1996, Jan. 1998). For second panel, survey by ABC News, May 1996. For third panel, survey by the Gallup Organization, April 1996. For fourth panel, survey by Market Strategies, Inc., June 1995.

TABLE 5–10
GOVERNMENT SUCCESSES, 1997
(percent)

QUESTION: I'm going to read a list of goals that the federal government has been working toward over the years, and for each one, I'd like you to tell me whether you think the government has been very successful, fairly successful, fairly unsuccessful, or very unsuccessful in working toward that goal.

	Very Successful	*Fairly Successful*	*Fairly Unsuccessful*	*Very Unsuccessful*
Promoting space exploration	44	41	6	5
Providing for the national defense	39	43	6	5
Keeping the nation at peace	33	47	9	9
Maintaining a growing economy	18	58	13	7
Protecting the environment	10	60	19	7
Supporting medical research	18	51	16	8
Making health care available to senior citizens	15	52	18	9
Regulating business to protect consumers and employees	11	53	15	13
Protecting the rights of individuals	13	50	19	14
Preventing discrimination based on race or sex	11	51	17	17
Supporting quality public education	13	36	25	22
Reducing poverty	5	27	33	30
Reducing crime	4	25	31	38

(Table continues)

TABLE 5–10 (continued)

	Very Successful	*Fairly Successful*	*Fairly Unsuccessful*	*Very Unsuccessful*
Improving moral values	3	26	29	36
Controlling illegal immigration	4	21	22	50
Reducing drug abuse	2	20	31	45

QUESTION: Over the past thirty years, how many significant successes do you think the federal government has had—a large number, a fair amount, just a few, or none at all?[a]

A Large Number	*A Fair Amount*	*Just a Few*	*None at All*
8	48	35	6

QUESTION: All in all, how good a job does the federal government do running its programs?

Excellent	*Good*	*Only Fair*	*Poor*
2	23	53	21

a. Those respondents who said there were a large number, a fair amount, or just a few significant government successes in the past thirty years (91 percent of the sample) were asked what the most important ones were. Eight percent mentioned the strong military and armed forces, 7 percent the space program, 7 percent welfare programs, 6 percent foreign policy, and 6 percent educational programs.
SOURCE: For first and second panels, survey by Hart/Teeter Research for the Council for Excellence in Government, February 1997. For the third panel, survey by the Pew Research Center for the People & the Press, October 1997.

TABLE 5–11
GOVERNMENT'S IMPACT TODAY, 1995–1998
(percent)

QUESTION: These days, what kind of impact do you think the government has on most people's lives—a positive impact, a negative impact, or doesn't the government have much impact on most people's lives?

	Positive Impact	*Negative Impact*	*Doesn't Have Much Impact*
Aug. 1996[a]	33	45	13
Sept. 1996[a]	32	42	16
Feb. 1997	28	41	22
Jan. 1998	31	40	22

QUESTION: Here are some reasons why people mistrust the government in Washington. For each one, please tell me if you agree, disagree, or are neutral about it . . . These are hard times in the country and the government unfairly gets the blame.

	Agree	*Disagree*	*Neutral*
1995	38	48	14

a. Registered voters.

SOURCES: For first panel, surveys by CBS News (Aug. 1996, Feb. 1997) and CBS News/*New York Times* (Sept. 1996, Jan. 1998). For second panel, survey by Market Strategies, Inc., June 1995.

TABLE 5–12
FEELING ABOUT THE WAY THE FEDERAL GOVERNMENT WORKS, 1992–1998
(percent)

QUESTION: I am going to mention four phrases and ask you which one best describes how you feel about the way the federal government works. Do you feel enthusiastic, satisfied but not enthusiastic, dissatisfied but not angry, or angry?

	Enthusiastic	*Satisfied*	*Dissatisfied*	*Angry*
Mar. 1992	1	17	60	20
Mar. 1992	1	21	54	23
Apr. 1992	1	20	55	24
June 1992	1	20	58	21
July 1992	1	22	53	23
Oct. 1992	1	16	56	25
Feb. 1993	4	29	50	16
Mar. 1994	1	29	48	20
Sept. 1994	2	25	53	20
Oct. 1994	2	24	53	19
Oct. 1994	1	26	52	20
Oct. 1994	1	25	55	18
Nov. 1994[a]	2	26	49	21
Jan. 1995	2	27	53	16
May 1995	3	45	41	9
Mar. 1996	2	27	54	16
Aug. 1997	2	33	52	11
Jan. 1998	2	43	45	8

NOTE: In a September–October 1997 survey, the Pew Research Center for the People & the Press asked people about government. Twenty-nine percent said they were basically content with the federal government, 56 percent said they were frustrated, and 12 percent said they were angry.

a. Registered voters.

SOURCE: Surveys by ABC News/*Washington Post*, latest that of January 1998.

TABLE 5–13

BEST GOVERNMENT IS ONE THAT GOVERNS LEAST, 1973–1996

(percent)

QUESTION: Now let me read you some statements some people have made about the way different levels of government should operate in this country. For each, tell me if you tend to agree or disagree . . . The best government is the government that governs the least.
QUESTION: Do you completely agree, mostly agree, mostly disagree, or completely disagree that the best government is the one that governs the least?

	Agree	*Disagree*
1973	32	56
1976	38	48
1981	58	36
1996[a]	61	39

a. Responses combined.
SOURCES: Surveys by Louis Harris and Associates (1973–1981) and the Gallup Organization (1996).

TABLE 5–14
Power of the Federal Government, 1941–1997
(percent)

QUESTION: Do you think there is too much power in the hands of the government in Washington? (Gallup)
QUESTION: Do you think the government in Washington has too much power or not? (Op. Dyn./Fox)
QUESTION: Now I'm going to read you a few statements some people have made about government . . . Do you completely agree, mostly agree, mostly disagree or completely disagree that the federal government is too powerful? (Pew)

	Yes	*No*
1941	32	56
1997	64	27
1997	62	37

QUESTION: Some people are afraid the government in Washington is getting too powerful for the good of the country and the individual person. Others feel that the government in Washington is not getting too strong. What is your feeling?[a]

	Government Not Too Strong	*Government Too Powerful*	*Don't Know or No Interest*
1964	36	30	34
1966	27	39	34
1968	30	40	29
1970	33	31	36
1972	27	41	32
1976	20	49	31
1978	14	43	43
1980	15	49	36
1984	22	32	46
1988	19	33	47
1992	17	40	43

(Table continues)

TABLE 5–14 (continued)

QUESTION: And what about the federal government, does it have too much power or too little power?

	Far Too Much Power	*Too Much Power*	*Right Amount of Power*	*Too Little Power*
1985	16	41	38	4
1990	13	35	47	4
1996[b]	24	40	29	3

QUESTION: Which of these statements comes closest to your view about government power today?

A. The federal government today has too much power.

B. The federal government is now using just about the right amount of power for meeting today's needs.

C. The federal government should use its powers even more vigorously to promote the well-being of all segments of the people.

	Poll	*Has Too Much Power*	*Using the Right Amount of Power*	*Should Use Power Even More Vigorously*
Sept. 1964	Gallup	26	38	29
Oct. 1964	Gallup	28	35	31
May 1978	ORC	38	18	36
June 1982	ORC	38	18	30
May 1984	Gallup	35	25	34
May 1985	Gallup	31	27	36
May 1986	Gallup	28	24	41
June 1992	Gallup	39	12	41
Mar. 1993	Gallup	39	27	31
Nov. 1997	Pew	33	32	33

a. Question wording varied slightly.

b. One percent chose response "far too little power."

SOURCES: For first panel, surveys by the Gallup Organization (1941) and Opinion Dynamics/Fox News and the Pew Research Center for the People & the Press (1997). For second panel, surveys by the University of Michigan National Election Studies, latest that of 1992. For third panel, surveys by the National Opinion Research Center, latest that of May 1996. For fourth panel, surveys by the Gallup Organization, Opinion Research Corporation, and the Pew Research Center for the People & the Press.

TABLE 5–15
FUTURE THREATS TO THE UNITED STATES, 1959–1995
(percent)

QUESTION: In your opinion, which of the following do you think will be the biggest threat to the country in the future—big business, big labor, or big government?

	Poll	Big Business	Big Labor	Big Government
1959	Gallup	15	41	14
1960	*Look*	15	41	14
1965	*Look*	16	28	37
1965	Gallup	17	29	35
1965	ORC	14	15	35
1966	Gallup	14	21	48
1967	Gallup	14	21	49
1968	Gallup	12	26	46
1969	ORC	12	17	44
1969	Gallup	19	28	33
1974	ORC	18	12	49
1976	Harris	11	15	33
1977	Gallup	23	26	39
1978	Gallup	19	19	47
1979	Gallup	28	17	43
1981	Harris	21	16	53
1981	Gallup	22	22	46
1981	Harris	22	15	52
1983	Gallup	19	18	51
1985	Gallup	22	19	50
1994	Roper/U. Conn.	14	5	67
1995	Gallup	24	9	64

NOTE: Question wording varied slightly.
SOURCES: Surveys by the Gallup Organization, George Gallup for *Look*, Opinion Research Corporation, Louis Harris and Associates, and the Roper Center for Public Opinion Research/University of Connecticut for *Reader's Digest.*

TABLE 5–16
GOVERNMENT CONTROLS TOO MUCH, 1987–1997
(percent)

QUESTION: Please tell me how much you agree with the following statement . . . The federal government controls too much of our daily lives. Would you say you completely agree, mostly agree, mostly disagree, or completely disagree?

	Completely Agree	*Mostly Agree*	*Mostly Disagree*	*Completely Disagree*
1987	18	40	32	5
1988	25	36	31	5
1989	22	35	34	9
1990	22	40	29	5
1991	32	31	28	7
1992	28	36	29	5
1993	26	39	30	4
1994	37	32	25	5
1996	23	40	31	7
1997	27	42	23	5
1997	29	35	29	6

SOURCES: Surveys by the Times Mirror/Pew Research Center for the People & the Press (1987–1994, 1997) and the Gallup Organization (1996).

TABLE 5–17
Confidence in Government Problem Solving, 1991–1996
(percent)

Question: When government in Washington decides to solve a problem, how much confidence do you have that the problem will actually be solved: a lot, some, just a little, or none at all?

	Poll	*A Lot*	*Some*	*Just a Little*	*None at All*
Oct. 1991	ABC/*WP*	7	31	38	23
Apr. 1992	ABC	4	46	38	12
Feb. 1993	ABC/*WP*	5	46	37	12
Jan. 1994	ABC/*WP*	4	39	40	16
May 1994	ABC/*WP*	4	31	42	22
Aug. 1994	Luntz	6	36	41	18
Dec. 1995	Kaiser	4	35	38	23
Apr. 1996	Gallup	4	35	39	21
Nov. 1996[a]	Luntz	6	35	42	15

a. Question wording varied slightly, asking respondents if they have a great deal, a fair amount, not very much, or no confidence at all.

Sources: Surveys by ABC News/*Washington Post*, ABC News, Luntz Research Companies, Kaiser Family Foundation/Harvard University/*Washington Post*, and the Gallup Organization.

TABLE 5–18
Government Creates More Problems Than It Solves, 1981–1995
(percent)

Question: Do you think that, in general, the federal government creates more problems than it solves, or do you think it solves more problems than it creates?

	Creates More	*Solves More*	*Both Equal*[a]
Jan. 1981	63	19	6
Jan. 1986	51	31	7
Jan. 1993	69	22	—
Dec. 1993	73	17	—
Mar. 1995	72	21	—

a. Volunteered response.

Sources: Surveys by CBS News/*New York Times* (1981–Jan. 1993), CBS News (Dec. 1993), and Hart/Teeter Research for the Council for Excellence in Government (1995).

TABLE 5–19
GOVERNMENT WASTE AND INEFFICIENCY, 1958–1997
(percent)

QUESTION: Do you think that people in government waste a lot of money we pay in taxes, waste some of it, or don't waste very much of it?

	Poll	*A Lot*	*Some*	*Not Very Much*
1958	Mich.	43	42	10
1964	Mich.	47	44	7
1968	Mich.	59	34	4
1970	Mich.	69	26	4
1972	Mich.	66	30	2
1974	Mich.	74	22	1
1976	Mich.	74	20	3
1978	Mich.	77	19	2
June 1978	CBS/*NYT*	78	17	2
Sept. 1978	*WP*	73	23	2
1980	Mich.	78	18	2
1982	Mich.	66	29	2
June 1983	*NYT*	69	26	3
Nov. 1983	*NYT*	74	21	2
1984	Mich.	65	29	4
Nov. 1984	CBS/*NYT*	67	27	3
Feb. 1985	CBS/*NYT*	69	25	3
Dec. 1985	*NYT*	75	21	3
1988	Mich.	63	33	2
Nov. 1988	CBS/*NYT*	71	24	3
1990	Mich.	67	30	2
Oct. 1991	ABC/*WP*	75	23	2
1992	Mich.	67	30	2
Oct. 1992	CBS/*NYT*	76	20	1
June 1993	CBS/*NYT*	86	12	1
Sept. 1993	Gallup	86	12	1
1994	Mich.	70	27	2
1996	Mich.	60	38	1

(Table continues)

TABLE 5–19 (continued)

QUESTION: Out of every dollar the federal government collects in taxes, how many cents do you think are wasted?

	Poll	*Mean (cents)*	*Median (cents)*
Nov. 1979	Gallup	—	40
Jan. 1981	Gallup	—	48
Apr. 1981	Gallup	—	40
May 1984	Gallup	—	45
July 1985[a]	ABC/*WP*	43	45
Feb. 1989	Gallup	—	50
May 1990	ABC/*WP*	46	50
Sept. 1990	ABC	44	50
Sept. 1990	*WP*	48	50
Oct. 1991	ABC/*WP*	49	41
Feb. 1993	ABC/*WP*	46	39
Aug. 1993	ABC/*WP*	47	40
Jan. 1995	ABC/*WP*	51	50
Nov. 1996	*US News*	49	—

QUESTION: For each statement, please tell me if you completely agree with it, mostly agree with it, mostly disagree with it or completely disagree with it . . . When something is run by the government, it is usually inefficient and wasteful.

	Completely Agree	*Mostly Agree*	*Mostly Disagree*	*Completely Disagree*
1987	19	44	27	4
1988	24	42	26	3
1989	26	39	26	5
1990	22	45	25	4
1991	32	36	23	7
1992	29	41	24	4
1993	24	45	24	5
1994	33	36	25	5
1997	27	37	27	7

(Table continues)

TABLE 5–19 (continued)

QUESTION: As I read each pair, tell me whether the first or the second statement comes closer to your own views—even if neither is exactly right . . . "Government is almost always wasteful and inefficient" *or* "Government often does a better job than people give it credit for."

	Government Wasteful and Inefficient	*Does a Better Job than Given Credit*
July 1994	66	31
Oct. 1994	64	32
Apr. 1995	63	34
Oct. 1995	63	34
Oct. 1996	56	39

a. Slightly different wording: Of every tax dollar that goes to the federal government in Washington, D.C., how many cents of each dollar would you say are wasted?

SOURCES: For first panel, surveys by the University of Michigan National Election Studies, CBS News/*New York Times*, ABC News/*Washington Post*, and the Gallup Organization. For second panel, surveys by the Gallup Organization, ABC News/*Washington Post*, and the Tarrance Group/Lake Research for *U.S. News & World Report*. For third panel, surveys by the Times Mirror/Pew Research Center for the People & the Press, latest that of 1997. For fourth panel, surveys by the Times Mirror/Pew Research Center for the People & the Press, latest that of October 1996.

TABLE 5–20
TRUST IN THE FEDERAL GOVERNMENT, 1958–1998
(percent)

QUESTION: How much do you think you can trust the government in Washington to do what is right—just about always, most of the time, or only some of the time?

	Poll	*None of Time*[a]	*Some of Time*	*Most of Time*	*Just About Always*
1958	Mich.	0	23	57	16
1964	Mich.	0	22	62	14
1966	Mich.	2	28	48	17
1968	Mich.	0	36	54	7
1970	Mich.	0	44	47	6
1972	Mich.	1	44	48	5
1974	Mich.	1	61	34	2
1976	Mich.	1	62	30	3
Feb. 1976	CBS/*NYT*[b]	5	55	29	7
Mar. 1976	Gallup	—	64	29	4
June 1976	CBS/*NYT*[b]	5	58	30	4
Sept. 1976	CBS/*NYT*[b]	4	52	35	5
Apr. 1977	CBS/*NYT*	3	62	29	6
Oct. 1977	CBS/*NYT*	2	62	28	4
1978	Mich.	4	64	27	2
Nov. 1979	CBS/*NYT*	3	64	26	3
1980	Mich.	4	69	23	2
Mar. 1980	CBS/*NYT*	2	69	22	3
Nov. 1980	CBS/*NYT*[b]	2	57	35	4
1982	Mich.	3	62	31	2
June 1983	*NYT*	1	46	43	7
Nov. 1983	*NYT*	1	51	38	6
1984	Mich.	1	53	40	4
Nov. 1984	CBS/*NYT*	1	51	41	4
Feb. 1985	ABC/*WP*	1	55	38	5
Feb. 1985	CBS/*NYT*	1	49	41	5
Mar. 1985	ABC/*WP*	2	60	32	5
July 1985	ABC/*WP*	3	58	32	6
Nov. 1985	CBS/*NYT*[c]	7	42	41	8

(Table continues)

TABLE 5–20 (continued)

	Poll	*None of Time*[a]	*Some of Time*	*Most of Time*	*Just About Always*
Dec. 1985	*NYT*	2	50	40	6
1986	Mich.	2	57	35	3
Jan. 1986	CBS/*NYT*	1	54	37	5
Sept. 1986	ABC/*WP*	2	58	34	6
Nov. 1986	CBS/*NYT*	3	46	42	7
Jan. 1987	CBS/*NYT*	2	52	37	7
Jan. 1987	ABC/*WP*	—	55	37	7
Feb. 1987	CBS/*NYT*	2	54	35	6
June 1987	ABC/*WP*	1	51	39	9
Oct. 1987	CBS/*NYT*	2	55	35	5
1988	Mich.	2	56	36	4
Jan. 1988	ABC/*WP*	2	59	34	6
Nov. 1988	CBS/*NYT*	2	52	40	4
Jan. 1989	CBS/*NYT*	1	53	38	6
1990	Mich.	2	69	25	3
Jan. 1990	ABC/*WP*	3	58	31	8
June 1990	Gallup[c]	11	47	36	6
Sept. 1990	ABC/*WP*	2	55	35	7
Oct. 1990	CBS/*NYT*	2	70	22	3
Nov. 1990	VRS[d, e]	8	57	29	3
Jan. 1991	ABC/*WP*	2	52	39	7
Jan. 1991	*LAT*[f]	17	54	25	3
Mar. 1991	ABC/*WP*	3	52	38	7
Mar. 1991	CBS/*NYT*	2	50	40	7
Oct. 1991	ABC/*WP*	5	58	28	8
Nov. 1991	ABC	—	70	24	4
1992	Mich.	2	68	26	3
Mar. 1992	*LAT*[f]	25	53	18	2
June 1992	Gallup	4	71	21	2
Oct. 1992	CBS/*NYT*	3	72	22	1
Oct. 1992	CBS/*NYT*	4	72	20	2
Oct. 1992	*LAT*[f]	22	57	19	1
Dec. 1992	CBS/*NYT*[d]	8	64	24	2
Jan. 1993	CBS/*NYT*	3	73	22	2
Jan. 1993	ABC/*WP*	5	67	23	5

(Table continues)

TABLE 5–20 (continued)

	Poll	*None of Time*[a]	*Some of Time*	*Most of Time*	*Just About Always*
Jan. 1993	*LAT*[f]	21	57	18	1
Feb. 1993	ABC/*WP*	4	74	17	4
Mar. 1993	Gallup	2	75	20	3
June 1993	*LAT*[f]	31	54	12	2
Aug. 1993	ABC/*WP*	3	72	20	3
Nov. 1993	ABC/*WP*	5	75	18	1
Dec. 1993	CBS[d]	13	70	15	1
Dec. 1993	*LAT*[f]	25	53	18	2
1994	Mich.	3	75	19	2
Jan. 1994	ABC/*WP*	8	68	21	3
Jan. 1994	Gallup	5	74	19	1
Jan. 1994	Gallup	—	80	17	2
Mar. 1994	ABC/*WP*	4	67	27	3
Apr. 1994	*LAT*[f]	30	55	14	1
June 1994	Gallup	9	73	14	3
Oct. 1994	ABC/*WP*	6	72	19	2
Oct. 1994	ABC/*WP*	4	75	18	2
Nov. 1994	CBS/*NYT*	2	76	20	2
Nov. 1994	VNS[d, e]	9	67	22	2
Jan. 1995	*LAT*[f]	21	60	18	1
Feb. 1995	CBS/*NYT*	4	77	16	2
Mar. 1995	ABC/*WP*	8	69	19	3
Apr. 1995	Gallup	—	78	18	2
Aug. 1995	CBS/*NYT*	4	75	17	3
Aug. 1995	Gallup	5	71	20	2
Aug. 1995	Gallup	4	73	21	2
Oct. 1995	*LAT*[f]	25	60	14	1
Nov. 1995	ABC/*WP*	6	67	22	3
Dec. 1995	Kaiser	4	71	21	4
1996	Mich.	2	69	26	3
May 1996	Gallup	4	69	24	2
May 1996	ABC	4	62	29	5
Nov. 1996	CBS/*NYT*	3	70	23	2
Dec. 1996	Pew	6	66	25	2
Jan. 1997	CBS/*NYT*	4	72	22	1

(Table continues)

TABLE 5–20 (continued)

	Poll	*None of Time*[a]	*Some of Time*	*Most of Time*	*Just About Always*
June 1997	Gallup	2	65	29	3
Aug. 1997	ABC	—	76	20	2
Nov. 1997	Pew	2	59	36	3
Jan. 1998	ABC/*WP*	3	66	27	4
Jan. 1998	CBS/*NYT*	3	71	23	3
Feb. 1998	Gallup	2	59	33	6

QUESTION: Would you say you basically trust the federal government in Washington or not?

	Basically Trust the Federal Government	*Do Not*
1997	39	57

NOTE: Some question wordings vary slightly.
a. Volunteered response.
b. Response category of "none" offered.
c. Response category of "almost never" offered.
d. Response category of "never" offered.
e. Sample is national adult voters leaving the polls.
f. Response category of "hardly ever" offered.
SOURCES: For first panel, surveys by the University of Michigan National Election Studies, CBS News/*New York Times*, the Gallup Organization, ABC News/*Washington Post*, ABC News, CBS News, Voter Research Service (ABC News, Cable News Network, CBS News, NBC News), the *Los Angeles Times*, Voter News Service (ABC News, Associated Press, Cable News Network, CBS News, Fox News, NBC News), Kaiser Family Foundation/Harvard University/*Washington Post*, and the Pew Research Center for the People & the Press.) For second panel, survey by the Pew Research Center for the People & the Press, October 1997.

TABLE 5–21
GOVERNMENT RUN BY BIG INTERESTS OR FOR BENEFIT OF ALL?
1964–1997
(percent)

QUESTION: Would you say the government is pretty much run by a few big interests looking out for themselves or that it is run for the benefit of all the people?

	Poll	*Few Big Interests*	*Benefit of All*
1964	Mich.	29	64
1966	Mich.	33	53
1968	Mich.	40	51
1970	Mich.	50	41
1972	Mich.	53	38
1974	Mich.	66	25
1976	Mich.	66	24
Sept. 1976	CBS/*NYT*[a]	57	33
Oct. 1976	CBS/*NYT*	61	31
Oct. 1976	CBS/*NYT*[a]	57	35
1978	Mich.	67	24
1980	Mich.	70	21
Nov. 1980	*LAT*[b]	50	41
1982	Mich.	61	29
June 1983	*NYT*	54	33
Nov. 1983	*NYT*	59	30
1984	Mich.	55	39
Nov. 1984	CBS/*NYT*	49	40
Feb. 1985	CBS	55	36
Dec. 1985	*NYT*	54	37
1988	Mich.	64	31
Nov. 1988	CBS/*NYT*	57	35
1990	Mich.	71	24
Sept. 1990	*WP*	51	38
Oct. 1990	CBS/*NYT*	71	21
Oct. 1990	CBS/*NYT*	77	18
Oct. 1991	ABC/*WP*	71	26
1992	Mich.	75	20
1992	Gallup[a]	71	23

(Table continues)

TABLE 5–21 (continued)

	Poll	*Few Big Interests*	*Benefit of All*
Mar. 1992	CBS/*NYT*	75	19
Apr. 1992	ABC	77	21
Apr. 1992	Gallup	80	16
1994	Mich.	76	19
Apr. 1995	Gallup	76	18
Aug. 1995	CBS/*NYT*	79	15
1996	Mich.	69	27
Nov. 1996	Gallup	64	29
May 1997	Gallup	74	22

QUESTION: For each statement, please tell me if you completely agree with it, mostly agree with it, mostly disagree with it or completely disagree with it . . . The government is really run for the benefit of all the people.

	Completely Agree	*Mostly Agree*	*Mostly Disagree*	*Completely Disagree*
1987	9	48	31	8
1988	11	42	34	10
1989	12	45	31	10
1990	10	42	35	10
1991	11	37	34	16
1992	8	36	37	17
1994	10	32	38	19
1997	9	39	35	15

a Registered voters.
b. Does not include phrase "looking out for themselves."
SOURCES: For first panel, surveys by the University of Michigan National Election Studies, CBS News/*New York Times*, CBS News, the *Los Angeles Times*, ABC News/*Washington Post*, ABC News, and the Gallup Organization. For second panel, surveys by the Times Mirror/Pew Research Center for the People & the Press, latest that of November 1997.

TABLE 5–22
SHOULD GOVERNMENT DO MORE OR LESS? 1985–1997
(percent)

QUESTION: Some people think the government is trying to do too many things that should be left to individuals and business. Others think that government should do more to solve our country's problems. Which comes closer to your own view?

	Poll	*Government Doing Too Much*	*Government Should Do More*
Jan. 1985	ABC/*WP*	57	38
Feb. 1986	ABC/*WP*	55	42
Jan. 1987	ABC/*WP*	49	47
June 1988	*WP*	48	49
Sept. 1990	ABC/*WP*	52	45
June 1992	Gallup	39	52
June 1992	ABC/*WP*	47	49
Aug. 1992	Gallup	50	43
Sept. 1992	Gallup	51	43
Sept. 1992	Gallup	46	47
Oct. 1992	Gallup	48	44
Mar. 1993	Gallup	45	49
Apr. 1993	Gallup	49	45
June 1993	Yank.	52	42
Dec. 1993	Gallup	55	38
Jan. 1994	Gallup	54	39
Oct. 1994	Gallup	57	37
Nov. 1994	Gallup	55	37
July 1995	NBC/*WSJ*	68	25
Nov. 1995[a]	Yank.	50	42
Dec. 1995	NBC/*WSJ*	62	32
Dec. 1995	Gallup	60	32
Jan. 1996	Gallup	58	35
Sept. 1996[a]	NBC/*WSJ*	58	34
Feb. 1997	Gallup	58	33
Dec. 1997	NBC/*WSJ*	51	41

NOTE: Some question wording varied slightly.

a. Registered voters.

SOURCES: Surveys by ABC News/*Washington Post*, the Gallup Organization, Yankelovich Partners, and NBC News/*Wall Street Journal*.

TABLE 5–23
GOVERNMENT OR BUSINESS AND INDIVIDUALS, 1992–1997
(percent)

QUESTION: Which comes closer to your view: "Government should do more to solve national problems" *or* "Government is doing too many things better left to businesses and individuals"?

	Poll	*Government Doing Too Many Things*	*Government Should Do More*
Nov. 1992	VRS[a]	41	49
Nov. 1994	CBS/*NYT*	63	30
Nov. 1994	VNS[a]	59	42
Nov. 1994	CBS	59	31
Jan. 1995	CBS	63	31
Jan. 1995	CBS	62	32
Aug. 1995	CBS/*NYT*	66	24
Oct. 1995	CBS/*NYT*	64	27
Feb. 1996	CBS/*NYT*	60	32
Apr. 1996	CBS/*NYT*	59	34
June 1996	CBS/*NYT*	57	36
Aug. 1996	CBS/*NYT*	58	36
Aug. 1996	CBS	60	32
Sept. 1996	CBS/*NYT*	62	28
Oct. 1996	CBS/*NYT*	62	29
Oct. 1996	CBS	57	34
Nov. 1996	VNS[a]	56	44
Feb. 1997	CBS	58	34

a. Sample is national adult voters leaving the polls.
SOURCES: Surveys by Voter Research and Surveys (ABC News, Cable News Network, CBS News, NBC News), CBS News/*New York Times*, and Voter News Service (ABC News, Associated Press, Cable News Network, CBS News, Fox News, NBC News).

TABLE 5-24
FAVOR LARGER OR SMALLER GOVERNMENT? 1976–1996
(percent)

QUESTION: Would you say you favor smaller government with fewer services, or larger government with many services?

	Poll	*Smaller Government with Fewer Services*	*Larger Government with Many Services*
Apr. 1976	CBS/*NYT*[a]	40	44
May 1976	CBS/*NYT*[a]	41	43
June 1976	CBS/*NYT*[a]	43	42
Sept. 1976	CBS/*NYT*[a]	48	38
Oct. 1976	CBS/*NYT*[a]	49	37
Nov. 1976	CBS/*NYT*[a]	44	44
Jan. 1978	*WP*[a]	40	39
June 1978	CBS/*NYT*[a]	53	36
Mar. 1980	CBS/*NYT*[a]	54	32
July 1984	ABC/*WP*	49	43
May 1988	CBS/*NYT*[a]	43	44
July 1988	ABC/*WP*	49	45
Oct. 1988	CBS/*NYT*[a]	45	38
Jan. 1989	CBS/*NYT*[a]	41	48
Oct. 1991	CBS/*NYT*[b]	42	43
July 1992	ABC/*WP*	55	38
Feb. 1993	ABC/*WP*	67	30
June 1993	*LAT*	60	29
Jan. 1995	*LAT*	63	27
Sept. 1995	*LAT*	62	27
Oct. 1995	*LAT*	68	23
Feb. 1996	CBS/*NYT*[b]	61	30
Apr. 1996	*LAT*	62	28
Aug. 1996	ABC/*WP*	63	32

a. Question wording was: "In general, government grows bigger as it provides more services. If you had to choose, would you rather have a smaller government providing less services or a bigger government providing more services?"
b. Question wording varied slightly.
SOURCES: Surveys by CBS News/*New York Times*, *Washington Post*, ABC News/*Washington Post*, and the *Los Angeles Times*.

TABLE 5–25
THE U.S. SYSTEM OF GOVERNMENT, 1992–1997
(percent)

QUESTION: Which of these statements comes closest to your views? "The federal government needs very major reform"; "the federal government is basically sound and needs only some reform"; "the federal government doesn't need much change at all"?

	Major Reform	*Only Some Reform*	*Doesn't Need Much Change*
1997	37	58	4

QUESTION: I'm going to read a few statements; for each, please tell me if you agree or disagree with it . . . Whatever its faults, the United States still has the best system of government in the world.

	Agree	*Disagree*
1992	85	14
1994	84	12
1996	83	15

SOURCES: For first panel, survey by the Pew Research Center for the People & the Press, October 1997. For second panel, surveys by ABC News, latest that of May 1996.

CHAPTER 6

Confidence in Institutions

In this chapter, we look at the responses to questions that three organizations ask about confidence in institutions. While other organizations ask about confidence as well, these three have the longest publicly available trends.

Poll users recognize the importance of question wording. In the confidence questions, Louis Harris and Associates asks respondents about confidence in "people in charge of running" various institutions. Harris asks if people have "a great deal of confidence," "only some confidence," or "hardly any confidence at all." The introduction to the National Opinion Research Center battery of confidence questions is similar: "I am going to name some institutions in this country. As far as the people running these institutions are concerned, would you say you have . . . ?" The response categories are identical to Harris's. The Harris surveys are telephone surveys; NORC uses personal interviews. Gallup asks, in contrast, about the institutions themselves: "Now I am going to read you a list of institutions in American society. Please tell me how much confidence, you, yourself, have in each one—a great deal, quite a lot, some, or very little."

In its comparisons over time, Harris emphasizes the proportions of those polled that say they have "a great deal of confidence" in institutions. The organization's 1997 press release, for example, did not report the responses of those having only some confidence or hardly any confidence at all, although those are available on request or on the organization's Web site. Gallup usually publishes all the responses, but news organizations that report on the findings tend to focus on those responding "a great deal" and "quite a lot." Not surprisingly, the picture produced by looking at Gallup's "a great deal" plus "quite a lot" responses is a more positive one than Harris's "harder" measure of "a great deal of confidence." Another factor that could contribute to the differing results we show here is that the polling organizations do not describe the institutions they are inquiring about in the same way. NORC and Harris ask about organized religion, for example, but Gallup asks about "the church or organized religion." In the appendix to this chapter, we explain the methodology that accompanies the confidence tables and identify the institutions.

In our commentary, we concentrate on changes in attitudes over the past twenty-five years. The Harris data take us back thirty years, but neither Gallup nor NORC had begun its series on confidence at that point. The final table shows the NORC 1996 rankings, Gallup's 1997 ones, and Harris's from 1998.

The Military. Our examination of confidence in core institutions begins with the military. Over the past twenty years, confidence in the military has edged up in both the Harris and the Gallup questions (table 6–1). Both Gallup and Harris show a drop in institutional confidence between 1996 and 1997, a development that may be related to the scandals that have received much attention of late, but Harris shows some pick up in early 1998. (The NORC General Social Survey, from which the confidence questions come, was not in the field in 1997.) Still, the military is one of the top-ranked institutions in American life today. As we look at these data and other polls about the military, it seems clear to us that the military's high standing in public opinion has much to do with the fact that the institution's mission of protecting and defending the nation is clearly defined in the public mind and, for the most part, the public believes it carries out that mission well.

Religion. NORC and Harris ask about organized religion; Gallup, about the church or organized religion. All organizations show a drop in the proportion expressing high confidence (table 6–2). Over the past thirty years, the number with a great deal of confidence in the church or organized religion in the Harris series has dropped almost by half. NORC finds a drop, too, but one that is not so dramatic. Gallup shows a drop of about ten percentage points over the past twenty-five years in the number with a great deal or quite a lot of confidence in the church or organized religion. Still, a majority, 56 percent in July 1997, told Gallup interviewers that they had a great deal or quite a lot of confidence in the church or organized religion.

The Press. In table 6–3 Gallup asks about newspapers, and NORC and Harris inquire about the press. Both the NORC and the Harris numbers show that confidence in the press was low initially and has dropped further. In 1979, Gallup reported that a bare majority had a great deal or quite a lot of confidence in newspapers; by 1997 that figure had dropped to 35 percent. For all three organizations, the number having low confidence has risen unevenly since these series began.

Television. From the beginning of each organization's series, people had less confidence in television than they had in newspapers or the press (tables 6–3 and 6–4). In the Gallup question of 1997, virtually identical numbers (slightly more than a third) gave newspapers and television news a strong vote of confidence. Only 10 percent in the latest NORC survey had a great deal of confidence in the people who run TV, and about twice as many in the Harris survey voice high confidence in those running television news.

Medicine. Table 6–5 looks at our confidence in medicine and the medical profession. NORC and Harris ask simply about "medicine." In 1975 and 1977, Gallup asked about medicine, too, but that polling organization dropped the category from the list of institutions it inquired about in 1978. Since 1993, Gallup has asked about "the medical system." Both NORC and Harris show a drop over the past twenty years in the number with a great deal of confidence in the people "running" medicine. Harris shows a small uptick over the period in the proportion having hardly any confidence. In the NORC question, that number has always been lower. In 1998, 36 percent in the Harris survey expressed a great deal of confidence in those running medicine; in the 1996 NORC survey, 45 percent expressed a great deal of confidence in that group. Both Harris and NORC showed a drop in confidence from their soundings in the early 1990s to their 1993 points, a time when the public was engaged in the debate about President Clinton's health care reforms. All three organizations show a small recovery in confidence since 1993.

Science. NORC has the only long trend on confidence in the people that run the scientific community, and the picture given by the data is fairly steady over the 1973–1996 period (table 6–6). In 1996, 39 percent had a great deal of confidence, 45 percent only some, and 8 percent hardly any.

Labor. Confidence in organized labor has not been very robust recently (table 6–7). In the Harris series, organized labor has consistently ranked very near the bottom of the institutions surveyed. The picture from the NORC in-person surveys is steadier than Harris's, although confidence is clearly low in both. Once again, Gallup's "great deal and quite a lot" responses produce a brighter picture. Still, only about a quarter of those surveyed by Gallup in the 1990s had a great deal or quite a lot of confidence in organized labor. All three organizations show that about three in ten have low confidence in organized labor.

Business. Gallup asks about big business, and Harris and NORC ask about major companies (table 6–8). Americans have long been skeptical about big institutions—big business, big labor, big government, and now big media. In its confidence in institutions battery in 1997, Gallup asked about big and small business. In 1997, 28 percent had a great deal or quite a lot of confidence in big business. By contrast, 63 percent had high confidence in small business. The preference for small over large is a familiar one in surveys. We also include here a question Roper Starch Worldwide has asked since 1978 to illustrate the point with respect to small and large companies (tables 6–9 and 6–10). In the 1973 Gallup survey, 26 percent had a great deal or quite a lot of confidence in big business; in 1997, 28 percent give that response (table 6–8). In 1973 in the NORC data, 29 percent had a great deal of confidence; the figure in 1996 was 23 percent. Harris found 27 percent with high confidence in major companies in 1973 and 28 percent voicing that view in early 1998. Around two in ten have hardly any confidence, according to the Harris data. Harris's measure of confidence in those running Wall Street, asked since 1977, finds that most people have "only some" confidence (table 6–11). In recent years, the numbers with a great deal of confidence and with hardly any confidence have been roughly the same. (On two occasions, in 1987 and 1988, Harris described this institution as the stock market.)

Banks. The savings and loan scandal in 1989 had a significant effect on professed confidence in banks and banking (Gallup) and in those running banks and financial institutions (NORC) (table 6–12). From 1988 to 1991 the number with hardly any confidence in banks more than doubled in Gallup's survey (from 11 to 25 percent), and in the NORC sampling it moved from 13 to 34 percent. The NORC data show some restoration of positive attitudes since then.

The Law. The number with a great deal of confidence in those running law firms has usually been lower than for any other institution, a finding that mirrors the generally negative attitude toward the legal profession shown earlier in table 3–14. In the Harris measure in 1998, 10 percent had a great deal of confidence, 48 percent only some, and 39 percent hardly any (table 6–13). Since 1993, Gallup has asked about confidence in the criminal justice system. Only about two in ten express a great deal or quite a lot of confidence, around 40 percent say they have some, and 40 percent have very little or none (table 6–14). In the mid-1970s, Harris asked about confidence in those running local police departments (table 6–15). From 1993 on, Gallup has asked about confidence in the police. Gallup's most recent measure for the police shows 59 percent with a great deal or quite a lot of confidence, 30 percent some, and 11 percent very little or none.

Education. NORC asks about those in charge of "running education"; Gallup asks about public schools. Both NORC and Gallup show a decline in their respective high confidence categories and a rise in low confidence ones since the early 1970s (table 6–16). In 1997, 40 percent in the Gallup survey had a great deal or quite a lot of confidence in the public schools, 39 percent had some confidence, and 20 percent very little or none. In the NORC measure in 1996, 23 percent had a great deal of confidence in those in charge of education, 58 percent had only some confidence, and 18 percent hardly any.

In surveys conducted since 1974 for the educational society Phi Delta Kappa, Gallup has asked respondents to grade the public schools in their community. In 1981, the organization began asking people to grade the public schools in the nation and, in 1985, to assess in the same way the school their oldest child attends. The results are shown in table 6–17. People are much more positive about the school their oldest child attends than they are about the schools in the nation. Table 6–18 looks at a Harris measure, asked since 1973, of people's confidence in those running "major educational institutions such as colleges and universities." (Those exact words were used for the first time in 1979; before then, the question asked about higher educational institutions.) In 1973, 46 percent said they had a great deal of confidence in these individuals; in 1998, 35 percent gave that response.

The Supreme Court. The Supreme Court seems to have held its own over the past twenty-odd years. Nineteen seventy-three was the first year all three organizations asked about the Court. In the Gallup poll, impressions of it have become slighly more positive over time; in the NORC surveys, they have been steady since 1973. Harris shows an uptick in confidence in 1998 (table 6–19).

The Executive Branch. Table 6–20 looks at NORC's and Harris's ratings of the executive branch of the federal government. Based on the number claiming hardly any confidence, NORC's picture of the executive branch is more pessimistic than Harris's. In 1996, 42 percent in the NORC survey had hardly any confidence in the executive branch of government. In the Harris survey from 1998, that figure was 21 percent. Only about one in ten says they have a great deal of confidence. Table 6–21 looks at Harris's rating of the White House and Gallup's more recent assessment of the presidency. The high point of confidence in the White House came during Reagan's presidency in 1984 (42 percent in 1984 said that they had a great deal of confidence), and the low point came in 1973, when 41 percent had hardly any confidence. In 1998, 18 percent said they had a great deal of confidence, 56 percent only some, and 24 percent hardly any at all. Gallup's question about confidence in the presidency is more recent, beginning in 1991. In that year 50 percent had a great deal or quite a bit of confidence; in 1997, that number was 49 percent.

Congress. We reviewed evidence of people's views about politicians and government in chapter 5. Gallup's confidence question shows a particularly sharp drop in the number with a great deal or quite a lot of confidence in Congress—from 42 percent in 1973 to 22 percent in 1997 (table 6–22). The number with very little or no confidence has almost doubled, from 14 to 27 percent. In the most recent NORC and Harris measures, only about one in ten has a great deal of confidence in those "running Congress." NORC, however, shows 43 percent claiming hardly any confidence in Congress (1996); for Harris that number is 19 percent (1998). Most major survey organizations ask regularly about approval or disapproval of the job that Congress is doing. We have not included these questions here. Viewed over the past two decades, these questions have generally revealed a secular decline in approval of Congress. The Gallup questions from early 1998, however, show a sharp improvement in Congress's standing.

Table 6–23 shows each organization's ranking of institutions we have shown individually in earlier pages. Congress tends to rank at or near the bottom of the lists.

Conclusion

Each of the tables on confidence tells its own story. But it is also important to draw general conclusions about our central social and political institutions. We have emphasized in our commentary the changes in positive ratings, as Gallup and Harris tend to in their own releases. For most institutions, the picture over the past twenty-five to thirty years is one of decline, although there are a few exceptions. For some of the institutions shown in these tables, the picture over the past twenty years has been steadier—although not wildly positive. There is some evidence that professed confidence is leveling off at low levels.

People's lack of high confidence in how central institutions are being run does not mean they have lost all confidence. Only about one in ten, for example, professes low confidence in the military. For a number of other institutions in the tables, only around two in ten have low confidence in their current operations. For many of the institutions, confidence bulks in the middle category. Again, though, the underpinnings of our democracy are strong. We are not facing a crisis in confidence, although we are dissatisfied with how many things are being handled. People want leaders to perform better, to stay on their toes, and to pay attention to popular concerns.

TABLE 6–1
CONFIDENCE IN THE MILITARY, 1966–1998
(percent)

	Gallup			*NORC*			*Harris*		
	GD/QL	S	VL/N	GD	OS	HA	GD	OS	HA
1966							62	28	5
1967							56	29	5
1971							27	47	20
1972							36	41	17
1973				32	49	16	41	35	18
1974				40	44	13	31	44	21
1975	58	25	12	35	46	14	30	42	21
1976	—	—	—	39	41	13	30	40	23
1977	57	25	13	36	50	10	28	49	17
1978	48	30	17	30	54	13	29	NA	NA
1979	54	29	14	—	—	—	29	48	18
1980	52	28	16	28	52	16	27	53	18
1981	46	34	16	—	—	—	27	54	17
1982	—	—	—	31	52	15	31	50	17
1983	53	29	13	29	55	13	33	54	11
1984	—	—	—	36	48	13	42	48	9
1985	61	28	9	—	—	—	31	50	18
1986	63	24	11	31	52	14	33	52	13
1987	61	28	10	34	50	12	33	49	15
1988	58	30	10	34	49	13	34	51	13
1989	63	37	—	32	50	13	30	54	15
1990	68	22	8	33	51	13	41	49	9
1991	69	20	9	60	33	6	47	40	11
1992	—	—	—	—	—	—	49	41	10
1993	67	23	9	42	45	11	55	38	6
1994	64	26	8	37	49	12	39	47	12
1995	64	27	8	—	—	—	43	44	12
1996	66	25	7	37	49	11	46	46	8
1997	60	27	12	—	—	—	36	49	13
1998							43	47	9

GD = great deal; QL = quite a lot; S = some; VL = very little; N = none; OS = only some; HA = hardly any; NA = not available.
SOURCES: See appendix to chapter 6.

TABLE 6–2
CONFIDENCE IN CHURCH OR ORGANIZED RELIGION, 1966–1998
(percent)

	Gallup			*NORC*			*Harris*		
	GD/QL	S	VL/N	GD	OS	HA	GD	OS	HA
1966							41	32	17
1967							40	27	15
1971							27	40	25
1972							29	40	22
1973	66	21	11	35	46	16	30	42	22
1974	—	—	—	44	43	11	32	40	22
1975	68	20	10	24	48	21	36	38	20
1976	—	—	—	31	45	18	24	42	24
1977	64	20	14	40	45	12	29	41	22
1978	60	24	14	31	47	18	34	NA	NA
1979	65	21	12	—	—	—	20	45	29
1980	66	20	11	35	43	18	22	43	32
1981	59	24	15	—	—	—	21	46	29
1982	—	—	—	32	50	15	20	48	27
1983	62	26	10	28	51	17	22	52	23
1984	—	—	—	31	47	19	22	48	26
1985	66	21	12	—	—	—	20	48	30
1986	60	27	12	25	50	10	20	48	28
1987	61	28	11	29	49	19	15	41	41
1988	59	27	13	20	46	31	18	49	31
1989	52	48	—	22	45	30	16	44	38
1990	56	26	16	23	49	24	20	49	29
1991	56	27	14	25	51	21	—	—	—
1993	53	29	17	23	50	25	—	—	—
1994	54	29	16	24	52	22	—	—	—
1995	57	28	13	—	—	—	24	—	—
1996	57	27	15	25	51	19	—	—	—
1997	56	28	14	—	—	—	21	52	24
1998							24	48	25

NOTE: See table 6–1 for abbreviations.
SOURCES: See appendix to chapter 6.

TABLE 6–3
CONFIDENCE IN NEWSPAPERS OR THE PRESS, 1966–1998
(percent)

	Gallup			*NORC*			*Harris*		
	GD/QL	S	VL/N	GD	OS	HA	GD	OS	HA
1966							29	50	17
1967							27	46	18
1971							18	51	26
1972							18	50	27
1973				23	61	15	28	53	17
1974				26	55	17	26	48	25
1975				24	55	18	28	47	21
1976				28	52	18	25	53	19
1977				25	57	15	18	55	23
1978				20	58	20	23	NA	NA
1979	51	35	13	—	—	—	27	54	17
1980	42	37	18	22	58	17	20	57	21
1981	35	42	20	—	—	—	16	60	22
1982	—	—	—	18	59	21	15	61	24
1983	38	41	19	13	61	24	19	63	17
1984	—	—	—	17	59	22	17	62	20
1985	35	42	21	—	—	—	15	60	24
1986	41	44	15	18	54	25	19	56	24
1987	31	46	21	18	56	24	18	56	25
1988	36	46	17	18	53	25	12	58	30
1989	—	—	—	17	54	27	17	58	24
1990	39	42	18	15	57	24	18	54	28
1991	32	44	22	16	54	28	14	56	29
1992	—	—	—	—	—	—	13	59	27
1993	31	42	25	11	49	39	13	63	23
1994	29	42	28	10	50	39	13	58	28
1995	30	44	25	—	—	—	11	51	38
1996	32	44	23	11	48	39	13	57	30
1997	35	43	22	—	—	—	11	58	29
1998							14	54	31

NOTE: See table 6–1 for abbreviations.
SOURCES: See appendix to chapter 6.

TABLE 6–4
CONFIDENCE IN TELEVISION OR TELEVISION NEWS, 1966–1998
(percent)

	Gallup			*NORC*			*Harris*		
	GD/QL	S	VL/N	GD	OS	HA	GD	OS	HA
1966							25	44	26
1967							20	44	26
1971							22	48	25
1972							18	51	26
1973	38	39	22	19	58	22	37	50	12
1974	—	—	—	23	58	17	32	50	17
1975	—	—	—	18	57	22	37	45	14
1976	—	—	—	19	52	27	32	52	13
1977	—	—	—	17	56	25	28	54	16
1978	21	37	40	14	53	31	35	NA	NA
1979	38	34	27	—	—	—	37	48	13
1980	33	39	26	16	55	28	28	55	16
1981	25	39	34	—	—	—	24	60	15
1982	—	—	—	14	57	27	24	54	22
1983	25	41	33	12	58	28	24	60	14
1984	—	—	—	13	57	28	25	58	17
1985	29	39	30	—	—	—	21	58	19
1986	27	41	31	15	56	28	25	55	19
1987	28	45	28	12	58	29	26	53	20
1988	27	44	28	14	58	26	17	57	25
1989	—	—	—	14	55	29	23	57	20
1990	25	41	33	14	58	27	26	57	16
1991	24	45	29	13	54	30	19	57	23
1992	—	—	—	—	—	—	21	56	24
1993	21	43	34[a]	12	51	37	20	58	21
1993	46	36	18[a]	—	—	—	—	—	—
1994	35	37	27	10	50	40	18	58	23
1995	33	41	25	—	—	—	14	48	37
1996	36	39	24	10	46	42	19	53	28
1997	34	42	23	—	—	—	16	55	29
1998							22	54	23

NOTE: See table 6–1 for abbreviations.
a. First point asks about television; the second about television news.
SOURCES: See appendix to chapter 6.

TABLE 6–5
CONFIDENCE IN MEDICINE OR THE MEDICAL SYSTEM, 1966–1998
(percent)

	Gallup			*NORC*			*Harris*		
	GD/QL	S	VL/N	GD	OS	HA	GD	OS	HA
1966							72	22	2
1967							61	27	5
1971							61	29	6
1972							48	36	12
1973				54	39	6	60	33	6
1974				60	34	4	49	38	12
1975	80	13	5	51	40	8	54	32	10
1976	—	—	—	54	35	9	42	43	12
1977	73	16	8	52	41	6	43	44	11
1978				46	44	9	39	47	11
1979				—	—	—	29	46	19
1980				52	39	7	35	49	14
1981				—	—	—	37	49	11
1982				45	46	7	31	50	15
1983				52	41	6	36	49	13
1984				51	42	6	43	48	8
1985				—	—	—	41	47	11
1986				46	45	8	35	49	12
1987				52	42	5	36	47	14
1988				51	42	6	40	48	11
1989				46	45	7	30	50	18
1990				46	47	7	36	50	13
1991				47	44	8	—	—	—
1992				—	—	—	29	50	20
1993	34	34	31	39	51	9	22	57	20
1994	36	38	26	42	48	10	23	52	23
1995	41	38	20	—	—	—	25	51	22
1996	42	38	19	45	45	9	27	54	18
1997	38	38	23	—	—	—	29	51	18
1998							36	48	15

NOTE: See table 6–1 for abbreviations.
SOURCES: See appendix to chapter 6.

TABLE 6–6
Confidence in the Scientific Community, 1966–1996
(percent)

	NORC			Harris		
	Great deal	Only some	Hardly any	Great deal	Only some	Hardly any
1966				56	25	4
1967				45	28	7
1971				32	47	10
1972				37	39	7
1973	37	47	6	46	37	6
1974	45	38	7			
1975	38	45	6			
1976	43	38	8			
1977	41	46	5			
1978	36	48	7			
1980	42	43	6			
1982	39	46	6			
1983	42	47	5			
1984	45	44	6			
1986	39	48	8			
1987	45	42	6			
1988	39	48	6			
1989	40	45	6			
1990	37	47	7			
1991	40	46	6			
1993	38	47	7			
1994	38	49	7			
1996	39	45	8			

Sources: See appendix to chapter 6.

TABLE 6–7
CONFIDENCE IN ORGANIZED LABOR, 1966–1998
(percent)

	Gallup			*NORC*			*Harris*		
	GD/QL	S	VL/N	GD	OS	HA	GD	OS	HA
1966							22	42	28
1967							20	38	29
1971							14	42	35
1972							15	44	33
1973	30	36	24	16	55	26	16	50	28
1974	—	—	—	18	54	25	19	46	31
1975	38	35	23	10	54	29	18	40	35
1976	—	—	—	12	48	33	10	47	36
1977	39	33	23	15	50	32	15	43	36
1978	20	31	43	11	46	38	13	43	34
1979	36	33	27	—	—	—	10	47	39
1980	35	34	24	15	50	30	14	52	32
1981	30	31	33	—	—	—	11	49	37
1982	—	—	—	12	53	30	8	50	40
1983	26	38	30	8	48	39	10	53	35
1984	—	—	—	9	53	36	10	52	36
1985	28	39	30	—	—	—	11	48	39
1986	28	39	29	8	47	39	9	52	35
1987	26	39	31	10	51	33	10	49	38
1988	26	40	31	10	50	35	9	53	37
1989	—	—	—	9	51	33	10	50	39
1990	27	40	28	11	53	31	12	56	30
1991	22	39	34	11	48	34	—	—	—
1993	26	41	29	8	53	32	—	—	—
1994	26	41	31	10	52	32	—	—	—
1995	26	46	25	—	—	—	8	NA	NA
1996	25	44	28	11	51	30	—	—	—
1997	23	43	29	—	—	—	9	56	33
1998							11	53	33

NOTE: See table 6–1 for abbreviations.
SOURCES: See appendix to chapter 6.

TABLE 6–8
CONFIDENCE IN BIG BUSINESS OR MAJOR COMPANIES, 1966–1998
(percent)

	Gallup			*NORC*			*Harris*		
	GD/QL	S	VL/N	GD	OS	HA	GD	OS	HA
1966							55	35	5
1967							47	32	6
1971							27	50	15
1972							27	44	21
1973	26	36	30	29	53	11	28	52	16
1974	—	—	—	31	51	14	16	48	33
1975	34	36	25	19	54	21	20	48	25
1976	—	—	—	22	51	22	19	51	23
1977	33	34	27	27	56	12	20	51	23
1978	27	38	30	22	58	16	23	55	17
1979	32	37	28	—	—	—	17	51	27
1980	29	39	28	27	53	14	16	54	27
1981	24	35	36	—	—	—	16	60	22
1982	—	—	—	23	58	14	17	60	20
1983	28	39	28	24	59	13	18	61	19
1984	—	—	—	31	57	9	21	58	18
1985	32	41	24	—	—	—	18	63	18
1986	28	40	28	24	62	10	17	60	20
1987	—	—	—	30	58	8	22	61	14
1988	25	42	30	25	60	11	16	60	23
1989	—	—	—	24	60	10	17	60	23
1990	25	40	31	25	61	11	15	68	16
1991	22	42	32	20	62	13	16	63	18
1992	—	—	—	—	—	—	11	63	24
1993	23	44	31	21	63	12	17	65	16
1994	26	42	30	25	61	10	20	59	18
1995	21	50	26	—	—	—	23	60	16
1996	24	46	28	23	59	14	21	59	18
1997	28	43	27	—	—	—	21	57	19
1998							21	58	17

NOTE: See table 6–1 for abbreviations.
SOURCES: See appendix to chapter 6.

TABLE 6–9
CONFIDENCE IN LARGE BUSINESS CORPORATIONS, 1978–1997
(percent)

QUESTION: What is your opinion of *most* large business corporations? There may be exceptions, of course, but would you say your opinion of *most* big business corporations is highly favorable, or moderately favorable, or not too favorable, or rather unfavorable?

	Highly Favorable	*Moderately Favorable*	*Not Too Favorable*	*Unfavorable*
Jan. 1978	14	48	22	10
June 1980	14	45	23	12
Nov. 1980	10	51	26	8
Jan. 1981	18	48	22	8
June 1981	16	49	21	9
Oct. 1981	14	46	24	12
Jan. 1982	23	45	20	10
June 1982	14	45	24	13
Oct. 1982	12	51	24	9
Jan. 1983	14	51	22	9
June 1983	20	53	18	7
Nov. 1983	18	50	21	8
Jan. 1984	17	54	20	6
June 1984	21	52	18	6
Nov. 1984	19	52	19	6
Jan. 1985	19	54	18	6
June 1985	18	53	18	7
Nov. 1985	20	50	17	7
Jan. 1986	21	51	16	7
June 1986	18	54	16	7
Oct. 1986	18	49	18	9
Jan. 1987	16	53	19	7
June 1987	15	52	20	9

(Table continues)

TABLE 6–9 (continued)

	Highly Favorable	*Moderately Favorable*	*Not Too Favorable*	*Unfavorable*
Oct. 1987	20	51	17	6
Jan. 1988	15	52	21	7
May 1988	16	53	17	8
June 1988	16	53	17	8
Oct. 1988	17	53	18	8
Jan. 1989	17	56	16	7
May 1989	15	57	16	7
Oct. 1989	15	55	18	7
Jan. 1990	15	52	21	8
May 1990	17	53	19	8
Oct. 1990	14	55	18	9
Jan. 1991	13	51	22	8
May 1991	13	51	22	8
Nov. 1991	14	50	19	10
Jan. 1992	13	50	23	9
June 1992	13	50	20	11
Oct. 1992	16	53	19	10
Jan. 1993	13	48	23	10
May 1993	14	52	19	8
Jan. 1994	16	52	19	8
May 1994	15	58	16	5
Oct. 1994	13	51	20	10
Jan. 1995	15	54	20	6
June 1995	17	52	20	7
Oct. 1995	9	53	22	9
Jan. 1996	12	54	22	7
Jan. 1997	15	53	21	6
May 1997	16	50	19	10
Oct. 1997	14	57	18	7

SOURCE: Surveys by Roper Starch Worldwide, latest that of October 1997.

TABLE 6–10
CONFIDENCE IN SMALL BUSINESS COMPANIES, 1978–1997
(percent)

QUESTION: Again, there may be exceptions, but would you say your opinion of *most small* business companies is highly favorable, or moderately favorable, or not too favorable, or rather unfavorable?

	Highly Favorable	*Moderately Favorable*	*Not Too Favorable*	*Unfavorable*
Jan. 1978	42	46	5	1
June 1980	42	46	6	1
Nov. 1980	35	55	6	1
Jan. 1981	46	44	5	1
June 1981	46	43	5	2
Oct. 1981	43	46	6	1
Jan. 1982	47	44	5	2
June 1982	43	48	5	2
Oct. 1982	41	52	4	1
Jan. 1983	48	44	4	1
June 1983	53	41	3	1
Nov. 1983	49	44	4	1
Jan. 1984	43	49	5	2
June 1984	56	37	3	1
Nov. 1984	48	45	4	1
Jan. 1985	49	44	3	1
June 1985	49	44	3	1
Nov. 1985	48	42	5	2
Jan. 1986	47	42	5	1
June 1986	51	40	4	1
Oct. 1986	51	39	4	2
Jan. 1987	46	45	4	1
June 1987	48	42	5	1

(Table continues)

TABLE 6–10 (continued)

	Highly Favorable	*Moderately Favorable*	*Not Too Favorable*	*Unfavorable*
Oct. 1987	49	42	3	1
Jan. 1988	49	42	4	1
May 1988	42	48	4	1
June 1988	42	48	4	1
Oct. 1988	46	45	4	1
Jan. 1989	45	45	4	1
May 1989	39	52	4	1
Oct. 1989	48	44	4	1
Jan. 1990	43	46	5	2
May 1990	48	43	5	1
Oct. 1990	42	49	4	1
Jan. 1991	40	48	6	1
May 1991	40	45	7	2
Nov. 1991	37	47	7	3
Jan. 1992	37	49	8	2
June 1992	42	45	6	2
Oct. 1992	46	46	4	1
Jan. 1993	38	46	9	3
May 1993	40	46	5	2
Jan. 1994	41	46	7	2
May 1994	37	50	6	2
Oct. 1994	40	48	5	2
Jan. 1995	36	50	7	2
June 1995	40	47	6	3
Oct. 1995	39	48	5	2
Jan. 1996	40	47	7	2
Jan. 1997	44	45	5	1
May 1997	41	47	7	2
Oct. 1997	39	50	7	1

SOURCE: Surveys by Roper Starch Worldwide, latest that of October 1997.

TABLE 6–11
CONFIDENCE IN WALL STREET, 1977–1998
(percent)

	Great Deal	*Only Some*	*Hardly Any*
1977	19		
1978	15		
1980	12		
1981	13	53	22
1987	12	59	21
1988	10	58	29
1989	8	58	30
1990	9	55	31
1991	9	57	26
1992	12	56	26
1993	14	63	19
1994	16	58	17
1995	14	61	19
1996	18	59	19
1997	19	57	17
1998	19	56	15

NOTE: See appendix to chapter 6.
SOURCE: Surveys by Louis Harris and Associates.

TABLE 6–12
CONFIDENCE IN BANKS OR BANKING OR FINANCIAL INSTITUTIONS, 1966–1997
(percent)

	Gallup			*NORC*			*Harris*		
	GD/QL	S	VL/N	GD	OS	HA	GD	OS	HA
1966							67	26	3
1967							54	32	5
1971							36	46	13
1972							39	44	11
1973							41	45	10
1975				32	54	11	42	42	10
1976				40	48	10	34	53	11
1977				42	47	9	40	47	10
1978	55	12	31	33	54	12			
1979	60	28	10	—	—	—			
1980	60	26	11	32	50	15			
1981	47	35	15	—	—	—			
1982	—	—	—	27	55	16			
1983	51	34	13	24	58	16			
1984	—	—	—	32	55	11			
1985	51	36	12	—	—	—			
1986	49	37	12	21	60	18			
1987	51	38	11	27	57	14			
1988	49	38	11	27	58	13			
1989	42	58	—	19	59	19			
1990	36	40	23	18	58	22			
1991	29	44	25	12	52	34			
1992	—	—	—	15	57	26			
1993	38	42	20	—	—	—			
1994	35	46	17	18	61	20			
1995	43	42	13	—	—	—			
1996	44	41	14	25	56	17			
1997	41	42	16	—	—	—			

NOTE: See table 6–1 for abbreviations.
SOURCES: See appendix to chapter 6.

TABLE 6–13
CONFIDENCE IN LAW FIRMS, 1973–1998
(percent)

	Great Deal	*Only Some*	*Hardly Any*
1973	20	55	19
1974	17	50	28
1975	16	50	26
1976	11	55	26
1977	13	53	27
1978	18	50	21
1979	15	55	24
1980	13	57	26
1981	16	58	23
1983	12	63	22
1984	15	59	22
1985	12	59	27
1986	13	59	25
1987	14	54	28
1988	10	54	34
1992	10	54	34
1993	9	53	36
1994	8	49	40
1995	8	50	41
1996	10	48	41
1997	8	54	36
1998	10	48	39

NOTE: See appendix to chapter 6.
SOURCE: Surveys by Louis Harris and Associates.

TABLE 6–14
CONFIDENCE IN THE CRIMINAL JUSTICE SYSTEM, 1993–1997
(percent)

	Great Deal	*Some*	*Very Little*
1993	17	38	43
1994	15	35	49
1995	20	37	42
1996	19	38	42
1997	19	40	40

NOTE: For the Gallup data above, the category "great deal" includes responses "great deal" and "quite a lot." "Very little" includes "very little" and, on some occasions, "none," a voluntary response. See appendix to chapter 6.
SOURCE: Surveys by the Gallup Organization.

TABLE 6–15
CONFIDENCE IN THE POLICE, 1973–1997
(percent)

	Gallup			*Harris*		
	Great deal[a]	Some	Very little	Great deal	Only some	Hardly any
1973				45	36	17
1976				37	45	16
1993	52	35	12			
1994	54	33	12			
1995	58	30	11			
1996	60	28	12			
1997	59	30	11			

NOTE: For the Gallup data above, the category "great deal" includes responses "great deal" and "quite a lot." "Very little" includes "very little" and, on some occasions, "none," a voluntary response.
SOURCES: See appendix to chapter 6.

TABLE 6–16
CONFIDENCE IN PUBLIC SCHOOLS OR EDUCATION, 1966–1997
(percent)

	Gallup			*NORC*			*Harris*		
	GD/QL	S	VL/N	GD	OS	HA	GD	OS	HA
1966							61	32	5
1967							56	29	6
1971							37	46	15
1972							33	46	16
1973	58	27	11	37	53	8	40	36	18
1974	—	—	—	49	41	8	—	—	—
1975	56	25	16	31	55	13	—	—	—
1976	—	—	—	37	45	15	35	46	15
1977	54	25	17	41	50	9	—	—	—
1978	45	30	22	28	55	15	29	48	19
1979	53	30	15	—	—	—			
1980	51	27	18	30	56	12			
1981	39	31	27	—	—	—			
1982	—	—	—	33	52	13			
1983	39	37	22	29	56	13			
1984	—	—	—	28	59	10			
1985	48	32	17	—	—	—			
1986	49	33	17	28	60	11			
1987	50	34	15	35	55	9			
1988	49	35	15	29	60	9			
1989	43	57	—	30	58	10			
1990	45	34	19	27	59	12			
1991	35	38	24	30	55	13			
1993	39	37	23	22	58	18			
1994	34	40	25	25	57	17			
1995	40	36	22	—	—	—			
1996	38	38	22	23	58	18			
1997	40	39	20	—	—	—			

NOTE: See table 6–1 for abbreviations.
SOURCES: See appendix to chapter 6.

TABLE 6–17
GRADING THE PUBLIC SCHOOLS' PERFORMANCES, 1974–1997
(percent)

QUESTION: Students are often given the grades A, B, C, D, and FAIL to denote the quality of their work. Suppose the public schools, themselves, in this community were graded in the same way. What grade would you give: the public schools nationally; the public schools here; the school your oldest child attends?

	Nation			*Community*			*Where Oldest Child Attends*[a]		
	A–B	C	D–F	A–B	C	D–F	A–B	C	D–F
1974				48	21	11			
1975				43	28	16			
1976				42	28	16			
1977				37	28	16			
1978				36	30	19			
1979				34	30	18			
1980				35	29	18			
1981	20	43	21	36	34	20			
1982	22	44	19	37	33	19			
1983	19	38	22	31	32	20			
1984	25	49	15	42	35	15			
1985	27	43	15	43	30	14	71	19	7
1986	28	41	15	41	28	16	65	26	6
1987	26	44	13	43	30	13	69	20	7
1988	23	48	16	40	34	14	70	22	5
1989	22	47	19	43	33	15	71	19	6
1990	21	49	20	41	34	17	72	19	7
1991	21	47	18	42	33	15	73	21	6
1992	18	48	22	40	33	17	64	24	10
1993	19	48	21	47	31	15	72	18	7
1994	22	49	23	44	30	21	70	22	7
1995	20	50	21	41	37	17	65	23	11
1996	21	46	23	43	34	17	66	22	11
1997	22	48	21	46	32	17	64	23	11

a. Asked of parents with children in the public schools.
SOURCE: Surveys by the Gallup Organization for Phi Delta Kappa, latest that of June 1997.

TABLE 6–18
CONFIDENCE IN MAJOR EDUCATIONAL INSTITUTIONS SUCH AS COLLEGES AND UNIVERSITIES, 1973–1998
(percent)

	Great Deal	*Only Some*	*Hardly Any*
1973	46	41	10
1974	39	44	14
1975	37	40	17
1976	31	47	17
1977	37	47	12
1978	41	NA	NA
1979	32	49	14
1980	35	50	13
1981	34	53	10
1982	30	54	14
1983	36	53	9
1984	40	52	7
1985	36	53	10
1986	35	50	12
1987	37	50	10
1988	37	53	10
1989	33	53	13
1990	37	52	10
1991	21	59	18
1992	25	55	19
1993	23	59	16
1994	25	56	18
1995	27	52	20
1996	29	55	15
1997	28	57	14
1998	35	51	13

NA = not available.
NOTE: See appendix to chapter 6.
SOURCE: Surveys by Louis Harris and Associates.

TABLE 6–19
CONFIDENCE IN U.S. SUPREME COURT, 1966–1998
(percent)

	Gallup			*NORC*			*Harris*		
	GD/QL	S	VL/N	GD	OS	HA	GD	OS	HA
1966							31	29	12
1967							40	29	21
1971							23	41	27
1972							29	42	21
1973	44	28	17	31	50	15	33	40	20
1974	—	—	—	33	48	14	35	44	17
1975	49	28	17	31	46	19	28	42	21
1976	—	—	—	35	44	15	32	43	21
1977	46	29	18	36	49	11	29	48	18
1978	39	32	21	28	53	15	27	47	19
1979	45	31	20	—	—	—	29	52	16
1980	47	30	17	25	50	19	27	53	18
1981	47	31	14	—	—	—	29	54	15
1982	—	—	—	31	53	12	26	54	17
1983	42	34	17	27	55	14	32	55	12
1984	—	—	—	33	51	12	38	51	10
1985	56	30	10	—	—	—	30	55	14
1986	54	33	10	30	52	14	35	53	10
1987	52	36	8	36	49	10	33	53	11
1988	56	30	12	35	50	11	33	56	10
1989	46	54	—	34	50	11	30	55	14
1990	47	31	18	35	48	13	35	51	13
1991	39	39	17	37	46	12	24	54	20
1992	—	—	—	—	—	—	30	54	15
1993	43	37	17	31	52	13	28	58	14
1994	42	38	17	30	50	16	34	51	14
1995	44	39	15	—	—	—	34	51	14
1996	45	39	15	28	50	17	33	52	15
1997	50	32	16	—	—	—	31	53	14
1998							40	47	12

NOTE: See table 6–1 for abbreviations.
SOURCES: See appendix to chapter 6.

TABLE 6–20
CONFIDENCE IN THE EXECUTIVE BRANCH OF THE FEDERAL GOVERNMENT, 1966–1998
(percent)

	NORC			*Harris*		
	Great deal	Only Some	Hardly little	Great deal	Only some	Hardly any
1966				41	42	11
1967				37	39	12
1971				23	50	18
1972				27	47	18
1973	29	50	18	13	42	41
1974	14	43	42	18	55	23
1975	13	55	30	16	48	29
1976	13	59	25	17	55	24
1977	28	54	14	23	56	14
1978	13	59	25	14	NA	NA
1979	—	—	—	15	62	18
1980	12	50	34	17	60	20
1981	—	—	—	24	57	17
1982	19	54	24	—	—	—
1983	13	54	29	—	—	—
1984	19	50	29	19	NA	NA
1985	—	—	—	20	60	18
1986	21	53	24	18	63	15
1987	19	52	27	19	59	19
1988	16	53	27	20	64	15
1989	20	54	22	18	66	15
1990	23	50	23	14	67	18
1991	26	51	21	35	53	10
1992	—	—	—	13	62	24
1993	12	53	32	15	66	17
1994	11	52	35	12	60	26
1995	—	—	—	10	66	23
1996	10	45	42	12	62	26
1997	—	—	—	12	67	19
1998				16	61	21

NA = not available.
SOURCES: See appendix to chapter 6.

TABLE 6–21
CONFIDENCE IN THE WHITE HOUSE OR THE PRESIDENCY, 1973–1998
(percent)

	Gallup			Harris		
	Great deal	Some	Very little	Great deal	Only some	Hardly any
1973				18	36	41
1974				18	52	27
1975				16	46	32
1976				14	53	29
1977				31	52	12
1978				14	NA	NA
1979				14	63	19
1980				17	56	23
1981				28	49	21
1982				20	55	23
1983				23	57	18
1984				42	41	17
1985				31	51	18
1986				20	59	20
1987				22	53	23
1988				25	57	18
1989				20	63	16
1990				21	59	19
1991	50	32	17	22	56	21
1992	—	—	—	15	61	23
1993	43	32	23	22	61	14
1994	38	34	27	17	56	25
1995	45	34	20	13	59	27
1996	39	40	19	14	57	28
1997	49	31	19	14	60	25
1998				18	56	24

NOTE: For the Gallup data above, the category "great deal" includes responses "great deal" and "quite a lot." "Very little" includes "very little" and, on some occasions, "none," a voluntary response. NA = not available.
SOURCES: See appendix to chapter 6.

TABLE 6–22
CONFIDENCE IN CONGRESS, 1966–1998
(percent)

	Gallup			*NORC*			*Harris*		
	GD/QL	S	VL/N	GD	OS	HA	GD	OS	HA
1966							42	46	7
1967							41	42	9
1971							19	54	19
1972							21	57	16
1973	42	36	14	24	59	15	17	56	24
1974	—	—	—	17	59	21	16	60	21
1975	40	38	19	13	59	25	12	49	33
1976	—	—	—	14	58	26	10	49	36
1977	40	35	19	19	61	17	17	54	25
1978	18	40	37	13	63	21	12	56	25
1979	34	39	24	—	—	—	18	58	20
1980	34	39	22	9	53	34	18	60	21
1981	28	45	21	—	—	—	16	63	19
1982	—	—	—	13	62	22	12	66	21
1983	28	42	25	10	64	23	19	65	14
1984	—	—	—	13	64	22	26	64	9
1985	39	42	17	—	—	—	16	66	17
1986	45	40	13	16	61	20	22	63	13
1987	—	—	—	16	63	17	20	57	22
1988	35	45	18	15	62	19	24	62	15
1989	32	68	—	17	58	22	15	62	23
1990	24	43	30	15	59	23	11	60	28
1991	18	43	36	18	53	26	8	56	35
1992	—	—	—	—	—	—	8	55	37
1993	19	40	39	7	50	41	10	56	34
1994	18	48	32	8	50	40	7	57	35
1995	21	48	30	—	—	—	10	68	21
1996	20	50	28	8	47	43	9	59	32
1997	22	50	27	—	—	—	11	67	20
1998							11	69	19

NOTE: See table 6–1 for abbreviations.
SOURCES: See appendix to chapter 6.

TABLE 6–23
RANKING OF INSTITUTIONS INSPIRING A "GREAT DEAL OF CONFIDENCE," 1996, 1997, AND 1998

Gallup 1997[a]	*NORC 1996*	*Harris 1998*
Small business	Medicine	Military
Military	Scientific community	Supreme Court
Police	Military	Medicine
Church/organized religion	Supreme Court	Educational institutions
Supreme Court	Banks & financial institutions	Organized religion
Presidency	Organized religion	Television news
Banks	Major companies	Major companies
Public schools	Education	Wall Street
Medical system	Organized labor	White House
Newspapers	Press	Executive branch
Television news	Television	Press
Big business	Executive branch	Organized labor
Organized labor	Congress	Congress
Congress		Law firms
Criminal justice system		

a. Ranking is the total of combined categories a "great deal" and "quite a lot."
SOURCES: See appendix to chapter 6.

Appendix: Methodology for Tables in Chapter 6

The following text reproduces the exact wordings for the Gallup Organization (Gallup), National Opinion Research Center (NORC) and Louis Harris and Associates (Harris) questions on confidence in institutions.

Gallup Question. "Now I am going to read you a list of institutions in American society. Please tell me how much confidence you, yourself, have in each one—a great deal, quite a lot, some, or very little?" (Note that for display purposes, we have combined the "great deal"/ "quite a lot" categories and the "very little" and voluntary "none" categories.)

In nearly all the years shown, the Gallup confidence question was asked only once. In the few years when it was asked more than once, the last point each year is used. On few occasions, Gallup included additional organizations in its battery. We chose not to use these as a significant trend was not provided.

The exact description of the institutions Gallup inquired about are the military; church or organized religion; newspapers; television (1973–1991, 1993); television news (1993–1997); medicine (1975, 1977); the medical system (1993–1997); organized labor; big business; banks and banking (1978–1991); banks (1993–1997); the criminal justice system; the police; public schools; the U.S. Supreme Court; the presidency; and Congress.

NORC Question. "I am going to name some institutions in this country. As far as the people running these institutions are concerned, would you say you have a great deal of confidence, only some confidence, or hardly any confidence at all in them?"

The exact description of the institutions NORC inquired about are the military; organized religion; the press; television; medicine; the scientific community; organized labor; major companies; banks and financial institutions; education; the U.S. Supreme Court; the executive branch of the federal government; and Congress.

Harris Question. "As far as people in charge of running (read each item) are concerned, would you say you have a great deal of confidence, only some confidence, or hardly any confidence at all in them?" (Note that in 1967 and 1972, the "hardly any" and voluntary "none" categories are combined.)

All the Harris percentages come from the Harris Center's database, with the following exceptions. Nineteen sixty-six and 1971 numbers are from a Harris poll summary in the *New York Post.* The 1977 and 1978 points for table 6–11 and the 1984 point for table 6–20 come from the 1996 Harris release. The 1978 points in tables 6–1, 6–2, 6–3, 6–4, 6–18, 6–20, and 6–21 come from Harris's 1997 release, as do the 1972 point for table 6–18, the 1980 point for table 6–11 and the 1995 point for tables 6–2 and 6–7.

The confidence numbers in the Harris Center database are unweighted numbers. We do not know if the data we refer to in the paragraph above that are not from the database are weighted or unweighted data. We have worked with Louis Harris and Associates in New York City and with the director of the Harris Center in North Carolina to try to present the fullest trends on these confidence questions.

In earlier surveys, Harris frequently included additional institutions. In most cases, confidence in the people running these institutions was measured only a few times, and we have therefore not included them. We have also used only the last point for each year when there were multiple askings.

The exact descriptions of the institutions Harris inquired about are the military; organized religion; the press; television (1966–1972); television news (1973–1998); medicine; the scientific community; organized labor; major companies; Wall Street (1977–1981, 1989–1998); the stock market (1987–1988); banks and financial institutions (1966–1972); banking (1973); banks (1975–1977); law firms; the local police department; education (1966–1972); local public schools (1973, 1976); schools (1978); higher educational institutions (colleges and universities and the like) (1973–1975, 1977); higher education (1976); major educational institutions such as colleges and universities (1979–1998); the U.S. Supreme Court; the executive branch of the federal government; the White House; and Congress.

CHAPTER 7

A Summing Up

As Americans see things, What's wrong? This question necessarily goes hand in hand with another—What's right? Let's begin this summary with the second.

The constitutional system is sound. For the most part, the U.S. public does not favor structural or institutional change. The core values that have constituted the United States as a nation remain firmly in place. Although many countries around the world are gripped by ideological upheavals, Americans are content with their country's historical social and political ideals. We believe opportunity is still present for us. What Herbert Croley called "the promise of American life," and what others have of late shortened to "the American Dream," is a promise of real opportunity for individual betterment, if effort is made. Amid predictions of a closing of the window of opportunity—not so common now as this volume goes to press but often heard over the past quarter century—Americans have at times given voice to concern. But we have continued to see a bright promise in our personal lives and, looking ahead, to those of our children. Where, then, do we see the problems?

Government is a problem. As noted, the basic political institutions are thought sound—and there is much we want government to do. Still, current performance is widely criticized. The reach of these criticisms helps explain why the public is now generally less receptive to calls for more government and more in favor of prudent curbs on government's role than in the years of the New Deal and the Great Society.

The "moral dimension" of national life is also an area where current performance leaves us troubled. Some of this dissatisfaction is but a manifestation of a long-standing nostalgic impulse.

"The good old days" had their fair share of problems—but those for the most part no longer occupy us. It is *today's failures* in civic life and ethical conduct—surely large and deeply troubling—that are, necessarily, front and center.

A wide range of national institutions—not just government but the press, the health care system, big business, and the schools—also suffer from relatively low and diminished public confidence in their leadership and current operations. This assessment is probably attributable partly to the harsh light that the press, especially its electronic arm, so often casts on them—but whatever the mixture of causation, professed confidence in the performance of many central institutions is low.

The authors of this volume have at times worried that commentary focuses too much on the sense of shortcomings in the management of national life and not enough on the many areas where Americans remain at once satisfied and confident. We hope this book will encourage a more well-rounded view. But we are aware as well that public dissatisfaction is essential to efforts at national improvement. Americans have a long list of specific candidates for what's wrong: those complaints are an important resource in pursuing carefully crafted reform.

APPENDIX

A Note on the Tables

We have grouped questions from different survey organizations together when they address the same subject. In chapter 2, for example, we have grouped several questions from different survey organizations about optimism and pessimism about the country's future. In chapter 5, we group together several survey organizations' questions on public officials' attentiveness to ordinary citizens.

On a handful of occasions, we include tables not discussed in the text. These tables are designed to provide the reader with additional data on the point we have been discussing.

In a few instances when a question was asked many times, we averaged responses. The question shown in chapter 3 asking whether the country is on the right or wrong track is one example,

We use dashes to indicate that a survey organization interrupted its asking of a question. If no dashes are present, the question was not asked. We also use dashes to indicate that a response category was not offered.

In some instances, percentages in the tables do not add to 100. In most cases, we are not showing the "don't know" or "no opinion" responses, and this is usually the explanation for the percentages adding to less than 100. For a few of the questions in this volume, small numbers of people volunteered a response that we have not shown and this is another reason we have used dashes.

Chapter 6 includes an appendix that provides detailed background information for the Gallup, Harris, and National Opinion Research Center questions on confidence.

About the Authors

EVERETT CARLL LADD is the director of the Institute for Social Inquiry at the University of Connecticut. He is also the executive director and president of the Roper Center for Public Opinion Research, a private, nonprofit research facility affiliated with the University of Connecticut since 1977.

Mr. Ladd's principal research interests are American political thought, public opinion, and political parties. Among his ten books are *American Political Parties: Ideology in America; Transformations of the American Party System; Where Have All the Voters Gone?* and *The American Polity* (all published by W. W. Norton).

An AEI adjunct scholar, he is a contributor to the *Weekly Standard,* a member of the editorial boards of four magazines, and the editor of the Roper Center's magazine, *Public Perspective.* In recent years, he has been a fellow of the Ford, Guggenheim, and Rockefeller Foundations; the Center for International Studies at Harvard; the Hoover Institution at Stanford; and the Center for Advanced Study in the Behavioral Sciences.

KARLYN H. BOWMAN is a resident fellow at the American Enterprise Institute. She joined AEI in 1979 and was managing editor of *Public Opinion* until 1990. From 1990 to 1995 she was the editor of *The American Enterprise.* Ms. Bowman continues as editor of the magazine's "Opinion Pulse" section, and she writes about public opinion and demographics. Her most recent publications include *Public Opinion in America and Japan* (with Everett Carll Ladd, AEI Press, 1996); *The 1993–1994 Debate on Health Care Reform: Did the Polls Mislead the Policy Makers?* (AEI Press, 1994); *Attitudes toward the Environment: Twenty-five Years after Earth Day* (with Ladd) (AEI Press, 1995); *Public Opionion about Abortion: Twenty-five Years after* Roe v. Wade (with Ladd) (AEI Press, 1997); *Attitudes toward Economic Inequality* (with Ladd) (AEI Press, 1998).

The American Enterprise Institute for Public Policy Research

Founded in 1943, AEI is a nonpartisan, nonprofit, research and educational organization based in Washington, D. C. The Institute sponsors research, conducts seminars and conferences, and publishes books and periodicals.

AEI's research is carried out under three major programs: Economic Policy Studies; Foreign Policy and Defense Studies; and Social and Political Studies. The resident scholars and fellows listed in these pages are part of a network that also includes ninety adjunct scholars at leading universities throughout the United States and in several foreign countries.

The views expressed in AEI publications are those of the authors and do not necessarily reflect the views of the staff, advisory panels, officers, or trustees.

A Note on the Book

This book was edited by Dana Lane
of the publications staff
of the American Enterprise Institute.
The text was set in New Baskerville.
Linda Humphrey set the type,
and Edwards Brothers Incorporated
of Lillington, North Carolina,
printed and bound the book,
using permanent acid-free paper.

The AEI Press is the publisher for the American Enterprise Institute for Public Policy Research, 1150 17th Street, N.W., Washington, D.C. 20036; *Christopher C. DeMuth,* publisher; *Dana Lane,* director; *Ann Petty,* editor; *Leigh Tripoli,* editor; *Cheryl Weissman,* editor; *Alice Anne English,* production manager.